T0097978

SECRET
GRANADA

César Requesens

JonGlez

We have taken great pleasure in drawing up
Secret Granada and hope that through its guidance
you will, like us, continue to discover unusual,
hidden or little-known aspects of the city.
Descriptions of certain places are accompanied
by thematic sections highlighting historical details
or anecdotes as an aid to understanding the city
in all its complexity.
Secret Granada also draws attention to
the multitude of details found in places that
we may pass every day without noticing.
These are an invitation to look more closely at
the urban landscape and, more generally,
a means of seeing our own city with the curiosity
and attention that we often display while
travelling elsewhere …

Comments on this guide and its contents, as well as
information on sites not mentioned, are welcome
and will help us to enrich future editions.

Don't hesitate to contact us:
• Jonglez Publishing,
  17, boulevard du Roi,
  78000 Versailles, France
• E-mail: info@jonglezpublishing.com

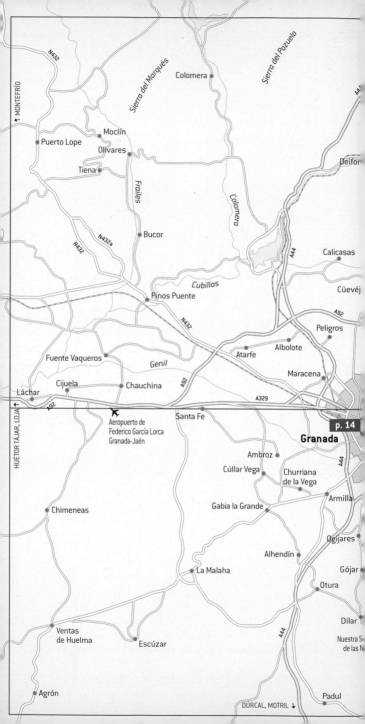

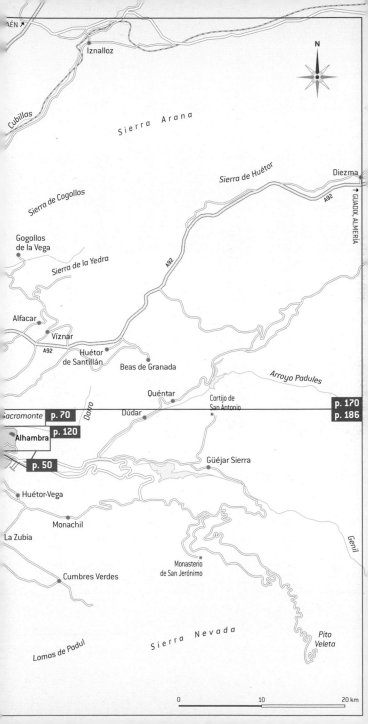

CONTENTS

OLD TOWN

REALEJO

ALBAICIN AND SACROMONTE

CONTENTS

CONTENTS

TO THE NORTH

TO THE SOUTH

OLD TOWN

PSYCHIATRIC WARD OF THE ALONSO CANO FACULTY OF FINE ARTS ❶

Aynadamar Building
Avenida de Andalucia, s/n
• Tel: 958 243 819
• www.bellasartes.org.es

Art therapy

The brand new Faculty of Fine Arts occupies the premises of what, for more than a century, was the provincial mental hospital. The small psychiatric ward still functioning within the same enclosure – the Granada North therapeutic community – is evidence of the former use of this large building. Patients receiving treatment here can be seen from time to time in the student cafeteria among the flamboyantly dressed aspiring artists studying in Granada.

The patients have full access to the faculty and likewise the students have free access to the hospital, symbolic perhaps of the close association between creativity and madness. The relationship between patients and students is harmonious. Indeed, this proximity has been studied within the context of the new discipline of art therapy. In this welcoming and calm environment, acute patients on the psychiatric ward have painted their own interpretations of works by artists such as Modigliani, Munch and Van Gogh.

The bars covering the large classroom windows, the deep corridors extending through the cellars and the numbering of the former patient bedrooms remind us that rooms used today for life drawing classes, sculpture workshops and/or artistic installations were previously used to alleviate the spiritual or mental distress of psychiatric patients from throughout the province.

In 2003 an exhibition entitled "Runaway Memory" was held in the Corrala de Santiago, presenting artworks in which patients from the therapeutic community reinterpreted the great masters.

REPUBLICAN COAT OF ARMS ❷

Façade of the former prison
Avenida de Madrid (next to Plaza de los Cármenes)

*Forgotten
Republican
emblem*

One of the rare vestiges of Franco's Spain in the city of Granada is the coat of arms that remains affixed above the principal entrance to the sinister former provincial prison, which no longer exists.

When Franco's regime came to an end, all Republican symbols were abolished by law. However, it seems that this coat of arms wasn't noticed by anyone for many years; no one knows why. Due to this oversight, it is ironic to think that many political prisoners taken to the prison at that time were received beneath the symbol of a Republic they had served loyally, costing them their freedom.

Only part of the main façade is still standing, and the coat of arms is the only reminder of those who were required to serve their sentences there. The prison disappeared when a new penitentiary was built in the nearby town of Albolote.

The former prison was included in 1985 (then excluded in 2001) in a catalogue of Granada's unusual buildings and buildings of artistic interest. The architect was Felipe Jiménez Lacal. Built of brick and with both classical and Mudéjar influences, the prison was demolished to open up a space in the heart of a newly democratic Granada. However, the door with its coat of arms remains. Its fine decoration and style saved it from disappearing, together with the large tower it supported.

The Republican coat of arms is very similar to the present-day Spanish coat of arms, except that it is surmounted by a crown made from towers, the heraldic symbol of the Second Spanish Republic. In 1931 it was decided to re-use this ancient composition, which includes the emblems of Castille, León, Aragón and Navarra, as we can see in this example in Granada.

PRISON RAILINGS IN PLAZA DE LA LIBERTAD

When the former prison was demolished, its outer railings were removed to a nearby square where – irony of history – the liberalist heroine Mariana Pineda was executed. In this way, the square today known as Plaza de la Libertad (Freedom Square), in memory of the heroic woman executed there, is now "imprisoned" by the railings of a prison that today lives on only in the nightmares of former prisoners.

ASSEMBLY HALL OF THE COLEGIO MÁXIMO ❸
DE CARTUJA

Faculty of Communication and Documentation (Library Sciences)
Cartuja university campus, s/n
• Tel: 958 246 252
• Open Mon–Fri 9am–2pm
• Contact the secretariat to arrange a visit

A secluded hallway of the Colegio Máximo de Cartuja hides what was once an enormous chapel when the Jesuits built this as the Faculty of Theology (see box).

An ancient chapel at the university

Today, the beautiful assembly hall of the Faculty of Library Sciences is an architectural gem which can be found at the end of many long corridors used by students rushing to and from their classes. The rectangular hall continues to transmit a sensation of peace from the times when young novices prayed here and gave their souls to God.

The hall is a haven of peace wrapped in shadows, as there is little natural light. What light there is filters through the windows, illuminating the gigantic, frescoed columns painted on the walls. The roof, which imitates the Mudéjar style, was covered with religious paintings. Today, the choir is a balcony where faculty professors and students hold meetings. Benches and kneelers from its days as a chapel have been replaced by countless chairs for those attending galas and conferences organised by the faculty. This magnificent hall is only used for major events.

COLEGIO MÁXIMO DE CARTUJA

The Colegio Máximo was established by the Jesuits as a novitiate centre in 1894. It was the first construction built in the Cartuja area, now the principal campus of the University of Granada.

Designed by the architect Rabanal, it reflects the taste of the era, with its historicist style. The structure is covered in bricks which create horseshoe arches in some areas. The principal façade is framed by two central towers with a sculptural group representing the Sacred Heart of Jesus, added in 1916.

This quadrangular complex is formed of four towers, four courtyards and towers that are four stories high (three in the intermediate structures). Purchased by the university for demolition in the 1970s, it remained abandoned for decades until the Ministry of Culture declared it a historical and artistic monument in 1983.

Instituto de Granada

Gen. *Ovis*
Sp. *aries* Monstruosho
Hab.

SCIENCE MUSEUM OF THE INSTITUTO PADRE SUÁREZ   ❹

Gran Vía, 61
• Tel: 958 893 120
• Open Mon–Thurs 10am–12 noon, Wed 5pm–7pm
• Guided tours
• Groups: max. 15 people under 13 years old and max. 20 people over 13 years old
• Entry fee. Reservation required

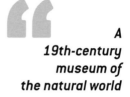

A 19th-century museum of the natural world

Since its establishment in 1845, the Padre Suárez Institute has been collecting curious objects, technological inventions and strange dissected animals that can be seen on the ground floor of the teaching centre.

In its early days, this may have been the best museum of scientific "rarities" in all of Andalucía, but it was forgotten for many decades. The rooms were only renovated in 1997, when an additional 4,000 exhibits from the natural world were added, including fossils, birds and mammals.

Nineteenth-century scientists were fascinated by the natural wonders on display: they include a sheep with six hooves and another with two heads. There is also a grisly human brain sliced into pieces so that all its parts could be seen and studied. There are technological inventions and curiosities such as a lovely collection of artistic kaleidoscopes from the 19th century, a magnifying glass and a magic lantern (the forerunner of today's cinema).

The collection also includes old scientific instruments for observation and analysis that allow us to understand Iberian fauna of the time, such as the bearded vulture and the Iberian lynx of the Sierra Nevada. The collections, which mostly date from the 19th century, are displayed in four rooms and a corridor. They give an overview of the work of early scientists in their attempts to catalogue and classify the order of the species.

The pioneer and moving spirit behind the collection was the university's first professor of science, Rafael García y Álvarez, famous for his work in propagating Darwin's theories in Spain. He prepared the first catalogue of the exhibits in 1886.

Professor José Taboada Tundidor continued this work, adding the collections of human anatomy stereoscopic cards and expanding the scientific material with the incorporation of microscopes, compasses and other instruments of the period. Currently, Professor Luis Castellón is continuing this long-term project of scientific divulgation, building on the selfless work of his predecessors.

NIVERSIDAD DE GRANA

EPARTAMENTO DE MINERALOGÍA Y PETRO

asificación Olivino (Pe

  cristal

ocalidad Gilgit (Paki

otación 3070

       Fecha

MINERAL MUSEUM OF THE DEPARTMENT OF ❺ MINERALOGY AND PETROLOGY

Faculty of Science, University of Granada
Avenida Fuentenueva, s/n
• Tel: 958 248 535
• www.ugr.es/ffminpet
• Email: minpet@ugr.es
• Open 9am–2pm
• Director of the museum: Prof. Fernando Gervilla Linares

*Exotic
stones*

The Faculty of Science at the University of Granada has an important collection of minerals. They are displayed in 21 well-lit cabinets in the central hall on the second floor of the Department of Mineralogy and Petrology.

The painstaking work of the Department of Geology, together with the chair of Crystallography, Mineralogy and Mineral Technology, have made it possible to collect, date and catalogue approximately 3,000 examples from the 1970s. Only some 1,300 are on public display, including more than 500 items from every corner of the world.

The exhibition is not particularly beautiful as its function is pedagogical, but it has some true rarities from various different parts of the Iberian peninsula: antimony and periclase from Málaga, nordstrandite from Haro, geikielite from La Coruña, carbonate-cyanotrichite from Beninar and pumpellyite from Antequera. It also has a fine collection of paragenesis and associated minerals from deposits in Tsumeb (Namibia), donated by the firm that mines them – they occupy pride of place in the exhibition.

Other important items in this small museum are galene from Herrerías (*quiroquita* variety), baryte from San Ginés de la Jara, Asturian fluorites and beautiful quartzes and agates from Brazil.

Most of the collection comprises the well-known gypsum, garnets, baryte and celestites from Spain and various minerals from the province of Granada. The provinces of Murcia, Andalucía, Ciudad Real and Badajoz have contributed ores, gangues and host rocks from deposits and even some surprising organic minerals, varieties of carbon and a selection of industrial rocks.

The current collection began with the purchase of 300 minerals, rocks and carbons in Germany at the end of the 19th century, for what was then known as the Department of Mineralogy of the University of Granada. The collection has been moved several times due to the changes of location of the Faculty of Science, resulting in the loss of various materials which have been replaced over time.

ALCOVE OF SAN JUAN DE DIOS

Basilica of San Juan de Dios
San Juan de Dios, 23
• Tel: 958 275 700
• Open Mon–Sat 10am–1pm and 3pm–7pm. Sun closed
• Suggested donation: 4€

The basilica's treasure

Catholics and art lovers alike will enjoy this small museum situated in the alcove of St John of God. It is found at the altar dedicated to the saint from Granada. His mortal remains can be seen here in a silver urn.

This "micro"-museum is divided into a sacristy, access stairway, antechamber, alcove and post-alcove, as well as being a space for recollection and silent prayer. Few of the churchgoers who come to mass every day in this well-attended church know of the existence of such a large quantity of works of art hidden behind the altar.

In this sacristy, a fragment of the bone of St John of God is kept in an inlaid urn, for veneration by the faithful. Tiles from Triana, ceilings painted by Saravia and Tomás Ferrer, a crucifix by Alonso Cano and a Holy Family by Risueño can be viewed from the access stairway. There is also a sleeping baby Jesus (18th century) resting in an alcove and, a little further on, a Madonna of the Incarnation painted on copper by the artist Becerril. Two 16th-century Chinese porcelain vases (Ming dynasty) take pride of place in the antechamber.

The alcove is resplendent with gold, silver and bronze. In the centre stands the silver urn (containing a wooden urn with the bones of the saint), surrounded by holy relics: the crucifix with which St John of God died, in his hands and on his knees, in the Casa de los Pisa; the *Lignum Crucis* (a piece of the Cross on which Jesus Christ was crucified); and a thorn from His crown, authenticated by Pope Benedict XIV.

Small bone fragments from all the saints in the history of the Hospitaller Order of St John of God (San Juan Grande and San Ricardo Pampuri, among many others) surround the urn. The walls of the alcove hold up to 123 crystal cases containing the remains of 1st-century martyrs, brought from the catacombs in Rome (such as San Teodoro and Santa Felisa).

The alcove used to be completely covered in silver, but during the French invasion of 1808, everything was lost … except the urn, which had prudently been hidden.

The space is extremely dazzling and baroque – perhaps too much so for modern tastes – but is typical of bygone eras, when a large number of saintly relics in a church served to increase its prestige.

LIBRARY OF THE FORMER FACULTY OF MEDICINE ❼ AND REFECTORY OF THE HOSPITALLER ORDER

Hospital of St John of God
San Juan de Dios, 23 (1st floor)
- Tel: 958 275 570 (San Rafael Hospital)
- Entry fee for the San Rafael Hospital
- Access upon request to the Brotherhood of St John of God

Secret library

On the first floor of the Hospital of St John of God, the superb yet little-known library of the former Faculty of Medicine is home to some real gems of medical history.

The reason why such a significant collection of old books is to be found in this forgotten site, in a suburban hospital clinic, is that the Faculty of Medicine was established in this building in 1857 and only opens its doors to very few visitors. The University of Granada trained doctors here until 1944, when the Faculty of Medicine moved to its current site in the Avenida de Madrid.

The smell of books is all-pervasive; they seem to have spent decades slumbering among the impressive shelves and the dust sheets. Some of the magnificent furniture dates back to a time when things were hand-made by skilled craftsmen, as shown by the inscriptions of King Ferdinand and Queen Isabella carved in the furnishings. All is silence, especially in a library that can only be accessed on rare occasions if one is fortunate enough to be admitted by the librarian for a short visit. The space is also used as a refectory by the brothers of the Hospitaller Order of St John of God.

The library is in one room of the Hospital of St John of God and is unashamedly baroque; it was originally the headquarters of the Jerónimos Order. It soon began to be used for providing assistance to the poor, which is why public access is restricted. During the visit, it is not unusual to run into patients who are recovering in the nearby private rooms.

NEARBY

REPLICA OF THE "SENTAÍLLO"

To the left of the entrance to the Hospital of St John of God is a niche with a small statue of Jesus in Meditation. Surrounded by ex-votos, the small Christ depicted there is a replica of the famous "Sentaíllo" (Seated Christ), a work by the school of Mora dating from the end of the 17th century and restored in 2006 by Dionisio Olgoso. The original image participates in the procession on the Wednesday of Holy Week in Granada and is carried by the Student Brotherhood from the Faculty of Law.

Both the original statue and this "mini"-Jesus in Meditation show Christ with a sad expression, his head resting on his right hand in a meditative pose. He is sitting on a large rock, which explains why he is known affectionately among the confraternities of Granada as the "Sentaíllo".

TOMB OF THE "GRAN CAPITÁN"

High altar of the church of the Monastery of San Jerónimo
Rector López Argüeta, 9
- Tel: 958 279 337
- Entry fee: 4€
- Open March–Oct: Mon–Fri 10am–1.30pm and 4pm–7.30 pm; Sat,
Sun and public holidays 10am–2.30pm and 4pm–7.30pm. Oct–March:
Mon–Fri 10am–1.30 pm and 3pm–6.30 pm; Sat, Sun and public holidays
10am–2.30pm and 3pm–6.30pm

Granada's "Great Captain"

At the foot of the high altar of the church of the Monastery of San Jerónimo, a niche is believed to hold the remains of Gonzalo Fernández de Córdoba y Aguilar, known as the "Great Captain" for his military expertise and various triumphs in the service of the Spanish crown (see box).

However, recent DNA analysis has revealed that these are not his bones. The tomb may have been plundered by French troops during the War of Independence (1808–1812), in response to the defeats inflicted by the great Spanish general on the neighbouring country.

The general's widow, María Manrique, the Duchess of Sessa, would visit every day to supervise the construction of the Monastery of San Jerónimo: it was to house her husband's remains after his initial burial in the Convent of the Barefoot Carmelites of San José. The street in which his wife lived during the building works, and along which she would walk to the monastery every day, is now known as Calle Duquesa.

Today, the tomb of the man who was once considered a hero is a solitary place, abandoned by the passage of time.

"THE GREAT CAPTAIN'S ACCOUNTS"

After years of brilliant battles in defence of the King of Naples, Gonzalo Fernández de Córdoba y Aguilar became known as the "Great Captain". With his knowledge of the highly effective combat techniques of the cavalry of Granada, he transformed the art of war by overcoming the immobility of the Middle Ages and making the infantry more agile.

The death of Queen Isabella I in 1504 distanced King Ferdinand II from Don Gonzalo, giving rise to the famous episode of "The Great Captain's accounts". The king accused Don Gonzalo of poor management of the funds he had been granted for the war expenses. The Great Captain responded with an exhaustive and detailed set of accounts. The Simancas Archive in Valladolid holds documents from the war in Italy: thousands of pages giving receipts and expenses, with details such as the name of each captain or sailor responsible for every item, which silenced any possible response from the monarch. The events were immortalised for history by the playwright Lope de Vega in his work *Accounts of the Great Captain.*

PLAQUE ON CALLE NIÑOS LUCHANDO ⑨

Calle Niños Luchando

> ### A stroke of luck with a bag of coins

The curious name, Street of the Fighting Children, derives from a fight that broke out between two brothers in a room overlooking this central Granada thoroughfare. The children were so involved in their frantic struggle that they knocked against a weak wall: it was unable to bear the weight of both of them and collapsed, causing a bag full of gold and silver coins to fall among the bricks and plaster. The father of the little boys, elated due to their unexpected good luck, commissioned a bas-relief for the façade of their house that (although later removed) depicted the scene of the children fighting which had brought such good fortune to that humble family of Granada.

OTHER STREETS WITH STRANGE NAMES

Calle Silencio

The name of this street (Silence), which runs from the Botanical Garden to the Faculty of Law, has remote origins in the city's Arab past. In the Nasrid period, it was located close to Bab al-Murdi, which is to say, the gate next to the orchard of Aben Murdi, meaning "son of the mute man". It is easy to understand how the word "Silence" gave its name to the street.

Calle de las Funerarias

The part of Calle San Jerónimo closest to the cathedral is known as the Street of the Undertakers, given the high number of funeral parlours located there at one time (there were as many as five). Currently, the only one that remains is the Funeraria Del Moral, near Plaza de la Universidad.

GHOST OF THE MUSIC PROFESSOR

Real Conservatorio Superior de Música Victoria Eugenia
San Jerónimo, 4G
Tel: 958 893 180
www.conservatorysuperiorgranada.com
Open during school hours

Strange noises, the inexplicable turning on and off of lights, and voices that whisper the names of professors when the centre is empty all challenge the scepticism of those who have worked and studied at the Royal Victoria Eugenia Conservatory of Music since the 1980s. In the central patio, in the calm and dead of night, strange gusts of wind rustling the leaves seem to open the way for a supernatural being.

The presence of a ghost was first noticed by Miguel Carmona, former director of the conservatory. It is said that the ghost is called Felipe and that he is a former music professor who was expelled from the conservatory after a lifetime devoted to music here. Despite being an experienced musician, the professor did not have the right qualifications. The ex-director is sure that, for years after his dismissal, the professor was consumed by a yearning for the conservatory that had meant so much to him.

These mysterious phenomena occur in a building that is filled with history. The conservatory has its headquarters in a charming palace in the city centre. It once belonged to the Marquises of Caicedo and, in previous incarnations, has also been a secondary school and the Faculty of Pharmacology.

NOCTURNAL ADORATION

Capilla de la Misericordia
Plaza de los Lobos, 12
• Open every day from 6pm
• Admission free

> *A whole night of prayer, so that the adoration of the Holy Sacrament continues non-stop*

Every day, from 6pm, the Chapel of Mercy receives the faithful who wish to pray at the same time as thousands of other Christians worldwide, during what is known as Nocturnal Adoration. This intimate ceremony is a strange contrast with the everyday noise of cars and pedestrians in Plaza de los Lobos.

Each member of this group commits to one whole night of prayer every month, so that the perpetual adoration of the Holy Sacrament continues without interruption. The objective of the Nocturnal Adoration is to pray together in shifts throughout the night – thus representing all of humanity – together with the "real" presence of Jesus in the Holy Sacrament.

The Holy Sacrament remains exposed during the simple, modest nightly ritual, accompanied by singing in Spanish and Latin, in imitation of Christ adoring the Father, in various passages from the Gospels.

The white banners with gold trim glisten in the baroque decoration of the chapel. Cherubs, Easter candles and various Marian devotions accompany this association of believers, established in 1848 (see box).

A CONGREGATION ESTABLISHED IN PARIS IN 1848

The Nocturnal Adoration Association was established in Paris in 1848 by Hermann Cohén, who was born in Hamburg in 1820. A Carmelite priest of Jewish extraction and a famous composer, he converted to Catholicism and adopted the name of Agustín María of the Holy Sacrament. The Catholic religious practice of Nocturnal Adoration was introduced to Spain by a Galician lawyer, journalist and politician of deep Christian faith, Luis de Trelles y Noguerol (1819–1891), after a journey to Paris in 1862 where he participated in a vigil. Subsequently, he devoted his life to spreading the practice throughout Spain, where there are currently a fair number of devotees.

INSCRIPTIONS IN THE CATHEDRAL

Façade of the Cathedral of Granada
Plaza de Alonso Cano

*Ancient
graffiti*

The inscriptions in the cathedral derive from a Roman tradition, adopted first by the church and then by the university and finally by Franco's regime: the names of eminent individuals are painted on the walls in red or black paint. The names on the façade of the cathedral are a kind of graffiti which traditionally indicated the names of the University of Granada's most illustrious scholars – those who were considered worthy of being remembered in perpetuity.

As a way of remembering and paying eternal homage, Franco's regime wished to continue with this custom, using a specific font that contained the letters V, C, R and T, thereby commemorating illustrious figures such as José Antonio Primo de Rivera (see box).

Today, the remaining inscriptions in the city are almost illegible and those on the cathedral walls are very difficult to make out.

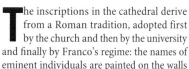

JOSÉ ANTONIO PRIMO DE RIVERA: PRESENT!

On one of the walls surrounding Plaza de Alonso Cano, we can read the name of José Antonio Primo de Rivera (founder of the Spanish Falange), in enormous letters. He was the ideologist of General Francisco Franco's fascist regime and the son of the early 20th-century dictator Miguel Primo de Rivera y Urquijo.

It is surprising to see his name, even though almost 40 years have passed since the establishment of democracy in Spain: during this time, various laws have ordered the removal of symbols of Franco's regime.

People nostalgic for fascism in Spain visit the cathedral walls so that they can pay posthumous homage to Primo de Rivera on three days a year: 2 January (day of the commemoration of the Fall of Granada to the Christian troops); 18 July (date of the military declaration against the Republic, previously known as Victory Day); and 20 November (anniversary of the death of Francisco Franco and of José Antonio Primo de Rivera).

There have been several attempts to erase this reminder of a time of conflict among the Spanish, but the name of José Antonio remains, as a memory of times that most citizens of Granada have already consigned to history.

BIRTHPLACE OF EUGENIA DE MONTIJO ⓬

Calle Gracia, 12

From Calle Gracia to Empress of France

The future Empress of France was born prematurely in Calle Gracia, in front of the Church of Mary Magdalene, in the neighbourhood of the same name. She was the second daughter of Manuela Kirkpatrick and Cipriano Guzmán Palafox y Portocarrero, Count of Teba, Marquis of Ardales and, later, Count of Montijo. She was born on 5 May 1826 in a tent pitched in the garden, due to an earthquake scare.

Currently the house, which is now divided into nondescript apartments, contains few reminders of its imperial history … with the exception of the façade, which is still decorated with the designs and architectural motifs that were so fashionable in the 19th century. A plaque by the door and a sign for tourists are the only reminders of the illustrious personality who once lived there, an ambitious local woman whose life reached great heights before her fall from grace.

RISE AND FALL OF AN AMBITIOUS WOMAN

Eugenia de Montijo's ambitious mother, Doña Manuela, was eager to show off her young daughter's beauty in high society in Madrid and Paris. Her father became the Count of Montijo when he inherited the title, possessions and entailed estate of an uncle who had died without heirs. Eugenia and her older sister, Francisca (Paca), were presented in society. Paca made an advantageous marriage with the Duke of Alba to spite her sister, who was in love with the same man. Following this disappointment, Eugenia and her mother left to try their luck at the French court. In Paris, the "belle Espagnole" caught the eye of Prince Louis-Napoleon Bonaparte (nephew of the great Napoleon). Taking advantage of his passion for her, she obtained the desired marriage and became Empress of France. Nonetheless, she suffered over her husband's numerous infidelities and her difficulties in providing him with an heir, and she was never a popular queen. Finally, Eugene Louis was born in 1857. In 1869 the Empress officially opened the Suez Canal together with the French nobleman Ferdinand de Lesseps. She was involved in political intrigue in support of Emperor Maximilian of Mexico and she acted as regent during her husband's absence. However, in 1870, after Napoleon III's defeat in the Franco-Prussian War and the fall of the Second Empire in France, she was surrounded by a mob in the Tuileries crying "Death to the Spaniard!" as the Paris Commune was established. During her inevitable exile in London, she mourned the death of her husband (1873) and her only son (1879), aged just 22. After her banishment, she died in the Palacio de Liria (Liria Palace) in Madrid in 1919. She was buried in London, far from her home, her family and the splendour of past times, when she was the shining star of a brief but glamorous moment in European history.

TOURS UNDER THE VAULTS OF THE DARRO RIVER ⓭

Granada Secreta
• Tel: 958 220 756
• www.granadasecreta.com
• Regular walks when reserved in advance with permission from the authorities • Duration: 3 hrs • Price: 25€ (plus equipment hire)
• Only for people without mobility issues

Urban speleology

The "Secret Granada" itinerary makes it possible to explore the subterranean route of the river that crosses the centre of the city, from Plaza Nueva to the mouth of the Genil River. Adventurers, specialists and curious visitors alike can discover a river where, until the 1950s, one could still see desperate yet somehow romantic prospectors panning for gold.

Equipped with wellies, helmets, torches and raincoats, visitors can explore the dark city depths under Calle Reyes Católicos, an engineering project which deprived the city of its principal artery in the name of progress.

The vaults over the river begin under Plaza Nueva, a symbol of the new era ushered in by the Catholic Monarchs (King Ferdinand and Queen Isabella)

when they unified Spain. This was the first stage of the vaults, completed in the 16th century in masonry over a wooden frame. The first section is dominated by riverside vegetation and is uncovered between the Rey Chico building and the start of the vaults, allowing a view of the Albaicín monuments and the Alhambra from an unusual perspective.

Some of the many bridges that linked people's lives in the Albaicín and the Alhambra still remain: the Puente de los Pescadores (Fishermen's Bridge), discovered in the 1990s; the Puente del Baño de la Corona (Crown Baths Bridge), built in the Nasrid period together with the public baths of the same name; and the Puente de San Francisco (Bridge of San Francisco) or Puente del Carbón (Bridge of Coal), which made it possible to cross the river between the Alcaicería and the Alhóndiga (Inn).

Another interesting discovery on this route is the Darro tanneries, where dyers would cut and dye leather (beneath Calle Tintes, or Dye Street). It is still possible to see the remains of large earthenware jars, some of which date from the 13th century.

At the end of the passageway, one can just make out a ray of light, which indicates the site where in 1951 the Darro burst its banks – the gushing water broke the vault above the river. Today the route of the river is marked by several waterfalls which make it possible to even the height of the riverbed with the difference in level between Plaza Nueva and the Genil River.

At the end of the route, the Genil appears luminous, striking the retina like a light at the end of the tunnel.

STATUE OF ISABELLA THE CATHOLIC

Above Teatro Isabel la Católica
Acera del Casino, s/n

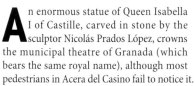

**A queen
standing
on the roof**

An enormous statue of Queen Isabella I of Castille, carved in stone by the sculptor Nicolás Prados López, crowns the municipal theatre of Granada (which bears the same royal name), although most pedestrians in Acera del Casino fail to notice it.

The sculptor (who was from Granada) was then working intensively on the projects that were to make him famous. He lived in an attic flat, just below the site of the statue, while the building works were completed.

The effigy was unveiled just a few days prior to the opening of the theatre on 6 June 1952. The first work presented there was Bizet's *Carmen*, which played to a full house of 1,200 – among the audience were the actors Joan Fontaine and Louis Jordan.

The Isabella the Catholic Theatre is located in Acera del Casino, just outside the city's largest casino (as the street name tells us). In spite of its size, the theatre did not really deserve its grand name – the acoustics were poor and the seats were uncomfortable. However, the structure is redeemed by Manuel Rivera's murals, which adorn the vestibule.

NEARBY

CENTRO ARTÍSTICO, LITERARIO Y CIENTÍFICO

2nd floor, Almona del Campillo, 2
• Tel: 958 227 723
• Visits by appointment

To the left of the Isabella the Catholic Theatre, we find the Artistic, Literary and Scientific Centre, a significant institution in the city. The centre's heyday was in the 1920s and 1930s, but it was losing its way until recent attempts to save it from closure and oblivion.

A group of Granada intellectuals established this institution in 1885; it developed from the Liceo Artístico and the Association of Watercolourists established by the painter Mariano Fortuny years earlier. In its second phase, starting in 1908, the centre was relaunched by a group of artists that included Manuel de Falla and Federico García Lorca. Among their many activities and projects, they promoted Granada's first Festival of Cante Jondo (a style of flamenco: literally, "Deep Song"), the Cabalgata de los Reyes Magos (Cavalcade of the Three Wise Men) and the Festival of Music and Dance.

HEADQUARTERS OF THE UNIÓN IBEROAMERICANA DE MUNICIPALISTAS (UIM) ⓯

Plaza Mariana Pineda, 9
- Tel: 958 215047
- www.uimunicipalistas.org
- E-mail: uim@uimunicipalistas.org
- Visits on request. Admission free

Defensive walls below the UIM

The remains of the three main walls that protected the city of Granada from invasions over the centuries can still be seen, almost intact, in a silent subterranean area beneath the headquarters of the Spanish American Union of Municipalities (UIM).

As you descend, you can see the remains of a bastion that protected the Roman, the Arab and later the Christian city on the site where the institution now keeps its archives. It is surprising to note how the various peoples who occupied this territory made use of the defensive walls built by their ancestors. The illumination of the three stone tiers, which were discovered by chance, allow you to see clearly how building materials were improved by advances in construction techniques or simply by refurbishing those already used with a layer of mortar to disguise their previous origins.

UIM

Established in 1991 through the efforts of various bodies in Granada, the Spanish American Union of Municipalities, also known by its acronym UIM, supports the links between towns in Spain and Latin America. It promotes the creation of more friendly and supportive communities through encouraging democracy, the decentralisation of power, and cooperation between civic governments acting as equals.

NEARBY

A NASRID TOWER: BIBATAUBÍN

Headquarters of the Consejo Consultivo (Inter-regional Advisory Board) of
Andalucía - Plaza de Bibataubín, s/n
• Tel: 958 029 300

In the same structure as the UIM, but just behind it, we find the impressive
Bibataubín building, currently serving as the headquarters of the Inter-
regional Advisory Board of Andalucía, although traditionally it was the
headquarters of the Provincial Government of Granada. Built in the 17th
century as a military barracks, it made use of an ancient octagonal Nasrid
tower which is still perfectly visible from the exterior of the building. This
tower formed part of the wall that protected Hispano-Muslim Granada
in the Middle Ages, just at the point where the city walls opened with the
Bibataubín Gate. Recently restored, its ground floor allows one to see the
magnificence of a Nasrid defensive tower from the interior. According to
legend, a subterranean tunnel connects it with the palace of the Cuarto Real
de Santo Domingo (Royal Palace of St Dominic) and its famous Qubba.

BUTTERFLY GARDEN IN THE SCIENCE PARK

Parque de las Ciencias
Avenida de la Ciencia, s/n
• Tel: 958 131 900
• Open Tues–Sat 10am–6.30pm; Sun, public holidays and Mon before a
public holiday, 11am–3pm
• Entry fee: 8.50€ (general), 5.50€ (reduced rate for pensioners,
children and groups), 5€ (students)

> *The world's largest butterfly*

The Butterfly Garden of the Granada Science Park is a lush tropical paradise that is well worth an extended visit. Butterflies that have broken free from their cocoons to enjoy a brief, ephemeral life flutter among the extensive vegetation for the enjoyment of visitors.

This is not just a paradise for entomologists to quench their thirst for knowledge. Children or artists with an interest in the natural world will be enchanted by this relaxing space, where you can enjoy wandering among the plants as if you were out in the wild together with the colourful, fragile butterflies. Many of the more than 200 examples – which come from Central America, South America and tropical Africa – are among the rarest species in the world. This is true of the most outstanding, the Attacus Atlas, whose extended wings can reach a span of up to 20 cm. Visitors to the garden can appreciate the complete life cycle of a wide range of butterflies. More than 20 varieties live in a privileged microclimate, with 70 varieties of tropical and subtropical plants, allowing them to feel at home.

The temperature, which is kept between 21° and 28° – with humidity of more than 70 per cent – allows caterpillars to eat well as they spin the cocoons from whence they will shortly emerge as butterflies and then lay their eggs. The life cycle of these insects – whose mysterious transformation surprises us with its immense beauty – is endlessly fascinating. Beginners and experts will learn about these lepidoptera which live in perfect symbiosis with their natural environment, so much so that the disappearance of a particular species of plant can destroy the corresponding species of butterfly that depends on it for sustenance. Visitors will also discover that 200,000 varieties have been identified (there are 4,000 in Spain alone) and marvel at the impressive migrations of some species, such as the Monarch Butterfly: every autumn they travel together from the north of the United States to Mexico or California, looking for the more temperate areas that allow them to survive. According to the data obtained from fossils, this butterfly dates back some 140 million years.

GRANADA'S CANDLE-CLOCK ⓱

Fundación El Legado Andalusí
Parque de las Ciencias
Avenida de la Ciencia, s/n
• Tel: 958 225995
• www.legadoandalusi.es
• Open Tues–Sat (and Mon before a public holiday) 10am–7pm; Sun and public holidays 10am–3pm
Closed Mon (except public holidays and the day before a public holiday), 1 and 6 Jan, 1 May and 25 Dec
• Free entry on 28 Feb (Andalucía regional holiday)

> *A strange clock to celebrate Mohammed's birth*

The Science Museum at the al-Andalus Pavilion of the Fundacion El Legado Andalusí is home to a curious scientific instrument. Described by the Arab historian, philosopher and poet Ibn al-Khatib (1313–1374), Mohammed V's candle-clock is full of symbolic significance whose inspiration lies in Arab hermeticism.

In his manuscript *Nufada III*, Ibn al-Khatib describes this clock (*minkan* or *mankana*), which was used to mark the hours during the Mawlid of the year 764 of the Hegira, corresponding to year 1362 of the Christian era. The Hegira is the period of the Prophet Mohammed's migration from Mecca to Medina. The Mawlid (*mawlid an-nabi* or *milad al-nabi*) is the date when Islam celebrates the birth of the Prophet Mohammed ... even though the Quran does not mention it and indeed advises against this celebration: "Do not exaggerate with regard to me as the Christians did with regard to the son of Maria. I am nothing more than a fearful servant of Allah."

Some Muslim theologians have opposed this practice over time as they do not consider it to be integral to Islam (*bida*, "innovation that leads to sin"). This celebration probably resulted from the influence of Christian celebrations of the Nativity of Jesus. Despite this theological opposition, thousands of Muslims celebrate the Mawlid with songs and prayers. In some countries there are parades and, over time, fireworks have become part of the tradition.

The specific role of Granada's candle-clock was to mark the hours of the celebration of the Islamic Nativity in the residence of Mohammed V (1338–1391). He was the Nasrid ruler of Granada from 1354 to 1359 and 1362 to 1391, and the first person to possess a clock that struck the hours of the night. Ibn al-Khatib details its mechanism in *Nufada III*: it was twelve-sided, made from hollow wood and stood 165–170 cm high. Each of its sides had a niche in the form of a mihrab, totally closed with a window with a bolt, and covered with polychrome decorations. A lit candle in the upper part was divided into twelve parts, one for each hour. A linen thread emerged from each section; twelve threads in total, each tied to one of the bolts, stopping them from opening. A hexagonal hollow in the tympanum of the arch of each mihrab served to drop a copper ball at the end of every hour, as well as holding an iron rod together with each bolt. Behind each window, the rod would stop the ball from dropping early. Each window also contained a figure holding a small sheet of paper that contained a verse, announcing the hour. When the flame consumed the candle and the hour reached its end, the linen thread would burn. This released the bolt holding the rod, thus allowing the ball to fall into one of the small copper trays. This made a loud noise at the same time as the small sheet of paper fell out with the verse for the hour, which would then be recited by a servant.

Over time, this clock – powered by the flame of a candle and by air moving through its hollow shape – provoked great curiosity. Whenever it has been tested, the mechanism is found to indicate the exact time, thereby demonstrating that its ingenious design remains reliable up to the present day.

Symbolically, the presence of the mihrab in the clock alludes to the sacred nature of time. (The mihrab is the niche in a mosque that indicates the direction, or *qibla*, of the holy city of Mecca, the direction towards which Muslims pray.) Moreover, the clock's twelve balls are made of copper, a metal that Arab alchemists associated with the planet Venus, considered the alter ego of the Moon, whose waxing crescent is the symbol of Islam. Thus, these ridged balls are symbolic of the Moon, whose craters are illuminated by the Sun, represented by the candle.

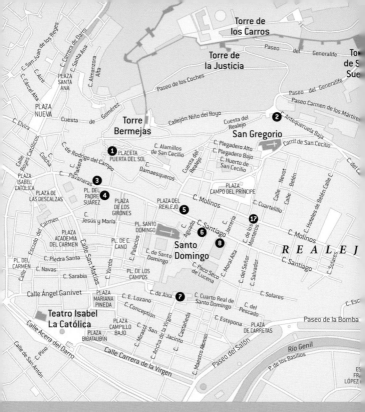

REALEJO

LAUNDRY IN PUERTA DEL SOL   ❶
Placeta del Sol

Washerwomen in the sun

The pavilion in placeta del Sol is home to a large rectangular stone that functioned until 1965 as a public laundry for the women of the local neighbourhood. In the past, when houses didn't have running water, something as basic as washing clothes was a daily ritual. This space allows passers-by to recall one of the most hidden areas of the Realejo neighbourhood.

As humble in its structure as the service it provided, the laundry is covered by an impressive roof with two streams of water, lending it the appearance of a temple. The roof is supported by thick columns of stone from Sierra Elvira, in the Doric style, taken from the remains of a nearby hermitage and incorporated in the structure centuries later.

Public laundries were in widespread use in Granada until the early 20th century. Many original laundries still remain and the smoothness of the stones is testimony to so many years of use.

The laundry, accessible only via steep passages leading up to the Mauror, dominates the entire placeta del Sol. Until 1501 this was the site of the Puerta del Sol or Bib al Mauror, the entrance from the Alhambra to the Jewish neighbourhood of Garnata Al-Yahud (Realejo).

AUDITORIUM OF THE ALHAMBRA PALACE

Hotel Alhambra Palace
Plaza Arquitecto García de Paredes, 1
• Tel: 958 221 468

**A little
theatre**

The interior of the Hotel Alhambra Palace features a charming theatre, which periodically presents a show or concert to the public. On special occasions it also hosts literary readings, following a tradition begun by Federico García Lorcain in the 1920s.

Classical recitals in this performance space began during the effervescent years of Granada's cultural explosion. Intimate concerts were hosted by Manuel de Falla (who wrote his *Antequeruela* in the neighbouring hotel) or the guitarist Andrés Segovia. Soloists and chamber music groups also perform in this very special theatre.

The arabesque decoration of the exceptional stage perfectly complements the performances of the International Festival of Music and Dance celebrated every year in Granada. Visitors can enjoy a fine concert together with tea or coffee during the afternoon or evening.

NEWSPAPER LIBRARY AT THE CASA DE TIROS MUSEUM ❸

Pavaneras, 19
(Entrance by calle Cementerio de Santa Escolástica, 3)
• Tel: 800 143 175
• Open weekdays 3pm-8pm (Aug 1 - Sept 15); 9am-2pm and 3pm-8pm
(Sept 15 - July 31)

A huge newspaper archive

For almost a century the Newspaper Library of the Casa de Tiros has accumulated a collection that has become a reference archive for all students of local history. It is the most significant collection in Andalucía and one of the most relevant in Spain, second only to the Municipal Newspaper Library of Madrid.

The reading room of this extremely significant library is located in the internal courtyard of a patrician home in the Realejo district. Here, it is possible to spend several hours in total silence, reading newspapers of many periods, especially those of the 19th and 20th centuries.

History unfolds day by day, brought to life by reporters with no time to gain perspective or reflect on the events they lived through. The collection is archived in the basement of the Casa de Tiros and is a valuable resource for

students of contemporary Granada.

Established in the 1930s in association with the Casa de Tiros museum on the initiative of the local Tourist Board, the original nucleus of the collection was greatly extended by regular updates. It is also based on thematic bibliographical collections associated with Granada and publications issued together with advertising and newspapers dating from 1706 to the present day. Some of the most important donations include papers belonging to writer and journalist Francisco de Paula Valladar, writer Melchor Fernández Almagro (including his correspondence with Federico García Lorca), the papers of Antonio Gallego Morell (concerning Ángel Ganivet and his father, Antonio Gallego Burín), and those of Ángeles Guerrero Ganivet, including photos and documents about Ángel Ganivet and the Seco family of Lucena, a family of journalists who donated the archive of the newspaper *El Defensor de Granada* to the Newspaper Library.

Of all the newspapers that have recounted the history of Granada, two have dominated public opinion during the last two centuries: *El Defensor de Granada,* established by the journalist Luis Seco of Lucena in the 19th century, and the newspaper that dominated the twentieth century, *Ideal,* which is more than 75 years old and still one of the most classic expressions of life in Granada.

BATHS AT THE COLLEGE OF MERCHANTS ❹

College of Merchants
Plaza Padre Suárez, 4
• Tel: 958 221 332
• Visits must be arranged with the college management
• Only small groups

Rediscovered baths

In 1984, during renovation work on the ancient palace of the marquises of Villalegre, a complete Arab bath was discovered in the basement of the College of Merchants. The thermal waters of the aristocratic building were protected over time by the builders of the palace who hid the discovery. Arches, columns, floors and even the stones that were heated to create steam were discovered when the chamber was finally opened. Archaeologists have dated the chamber to the Almohad period, between the 12th and 13th centuries.

Accessed through a trap door in the floor, the square space is built in brick and surrounded by columns of stone supporting iron arches over a marble floor. It follows the typical structure of Roman baths with a *tepidarium, caldarium, frigidarium* and *hipocaustum,* although visitors can only enter the *tepidarium* (the central area) and two of the passages around the bath.

In the nearby Alacena de las Monjas restaurant we find the ancient well that provided water to these baths, located (according to Islamic custom) in the mosque of Ibn Gimara, today found in the same building as the Casa de los Tiros.

OTHER INACCESSIBLE BATHS

In Granada there are various baths from the period of Arab domination that are not open to visitors, although renovation works are at an advanced stage, such as the Tumbas Baths (Elvira Gate) and the Baths in calle del Agua (Albaicín), which have significant archaeological and cultural value. However, one can visit the Bañuelo Baths in the Carrera del Darro, the Baths of the Alhambra, or the Polinario Baths at the Museum of the Ángel neighbourhood in Calle Real del Alhambra.

NEARBY

ENTRANCE TO THE PALACE OF THE COUNTS OF CASTILLEJO IN CHAFLÁN
Ballesteros, 8

Dating from the early 16th century, the entrance to the Palace of the Counts of Castillejo in Chaflán is remarkable due to its architectural oddities as well as the coat of arms flanked by two dragons over the main door. For many years it was known locally as the House of Diego de Siloé, although it has not been possible to determine its relationship to the architect of the cathedral.

SANTIAGO STREET TENEMENT

Santiago, 5
- Tel: 958 220 527
- http://corraladesantiago.ugr.es/
- Open: Mon-Sun 10am-8pm
- Entry free

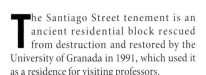

The Santiago Street tenement is an ancient residential block rescued from destruction and restored by the University of Granada in 1991, which used it as a residence for visiting professors.

An old residential courtyard

These residential blocks, of which there are very few examples left in Granada, were used by the working class until the middle of the last century when modern structures were built in outlying areas. The constructions provide an insight into daily life in the city between the 16th and 17th centuries. Some even remained in use until relatively recently.

The central patio was the focal point of life in the building, a place to meet and chat, collect water from the fountain or well, or indeed to wash clothes in the basins located against a wall or in the centre.

The Santiago Street tenement consists of a ground floor with "rooms" or apartments and upper floors of apartments. With little decoration other than some wooden pillars, columns or coloured skirting boards, the interior and façade of this type of home reflect the humble condition of the inhabitants and the communal character of its residents' lifestyle. Although originally built as housing for the city's working class (bricklayers, blacksmiths, carpenters, maids), all neighbours would come together for weddings, baptisms, funerals or first communions, regardless of any domestic disputes.

Tenements are based on the designs of earlier Arab constructions known as *adarves* (alleyways with a single entrance), particularly the Mozarabic 'curralaz' (corral), which have existed since the 14th century.

The remote origins of some tenements can be found in patrician homes, convents or *alhóndigas* (homes of travellers and merchants), which were adapted from their original usage to house as many families as possible.

BEGINNING OF THE MOZARABIC ROUTE TO SANTIAGO ❻

Convent of Commanders of Santiago
Plaza Ciudad de los Cármenes, 1 (Centro Cívico Beiro)
Association of Friends of the Mozarabic route to Santiago
• Tel: 958 071 785-655010 605
• E-mail: info@eliniciomozarabe.es
• www.eliniciomozarabe.es
• Open: Tue-Thurs (not bank holidays) 6pm-9pm

Perhaps the least known of all routes to Santiago

The Christians of Al-Ándalus (Mozarabites) traveled this route to make their pilgrimage to the sepulchre of the Apostol Saint James.

Today, some still walk the 1,200 kilometres from Granada to Santiago.

The route, which crosses south-east Spain to Mérida, is perhaps the least known of all routes to Santiago. It also provides access to the Silver Route, which links Cádiz and Seville with Santiago.

Forgotten for centuries, it was given new life in the spring of 1994 when Jesuit priest Father Hermenegildo del Campa travelled from Granada with a small group of pilgrims to visit the tomb of the Apostle, an experience he recounts in *De Granada a Santiago, una ruta jacobea andaluza.*

Setting out from the convent of the Commanders of Santiago in the Realejo district, the pilgrims walk through Granada, Maracena and Atarfe, spending their first night in Pinos Puente, where the first hostel for pilgrims of the province of Granada, known as "El plantel" (see box), was recently opened.

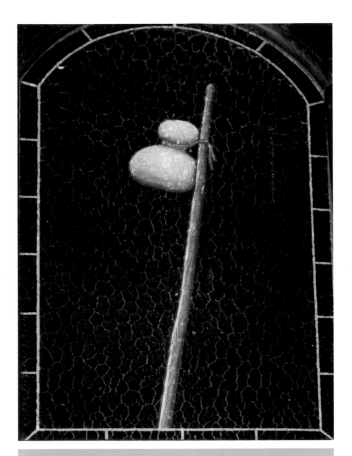

THE FIRST HOSTEL

In 2012 the first hostel for pilgrims along the Jacobea route from Granada opened in Pinos Puente. Here, it is possible to see the ancient bridge dating from the 9th century, which gives its name to the village. The hostel is the first structure of its kind between Granada and Mérida. It is owned by the municipal government and managed by the Granada Jacobea Association, which has spent the last decade sign-posting and upgrading the route to the extent that it is now better known in Finland, Holland and Italy than in Granada.

ROYAL CHAMBER OF SAINT DOMINIC

Plaza de los Campos, s/n
• Open: Wed-Sun 10am-2pm and 5pm-8pm (May-Sept); Fri-Sun 10am-2pm and 4pm-6pm (Oct-Apr)

*A palace
for the soul*

I n the corner of the plaza de los Campos we find the Royal Chamber of Saint Dominic. This 19th-century mansion built around an Almohad structure incorporates the *Qubba*, a large tower also known as the "Meeting Room".

Between children's voices rising from the Japanese gardens and the quiet of the nearby Commanders of Santiago, this charming space was used as a spiritual retreat by past monarchs. It was also the location chosen by the Muslim kings of Granada in which to fast during the month of Ramadan.

The large impressive central tower and jewel of the building is an integral part of the ancient Alfarero city walls and comprises both a central salon and two lateral alcoves.

It is perhaps easier to appreciate from calle de Aixa, where it is possible to see how the entire building has gradually been absorbed by construction over the years.

For eight centuries, the elaborately decorated Mozarabite, with its exquisite marble and ornamental tiles, heard the prayers of the chamber's illustrious inhabitants. The fountain (the last remnants of an ancient pond in the garden), the layers of wood in the alcove and the window in the room to the right are the only other remains that hint at the splendour of the past.

With the decline of Al Ándalus, the palace was purchased by King Ferdinand and Queen Isabella for members of the royal family. It was later given to the Dominican Order, forming part of the complex that includes the church of Saint Dominic and the ancient Convent of Santa Cruz Royal (today a secondary school).

Following the disentailment of Mendizábal, it fell into private hands until it was purchased by the Town Hall in order to restore the *Qubba* and the gardens.

LUNCH IN THE ROYAL MONASTERY OF THE MOTHER OF GOD OF THE COMMANDERS OF SANTIAGO ⑧

Seco of Lucena, s/n
• Tel: 958 225 250
• E-mail: comendadorasdesantiagogranada@gmail.com
• Closed in August
• Menu: 11€ (reservations required for lunch)
• Overnight stay: 40€ per person/day

Very hospitable nuns

The guesthouse of the Convent of the Commanders of Santiago is an enormous complex dedicated to the contemplation and work of approximately twenty nuns, mainly from India, who live a semi-cloistered existence at the very heart of the Realejo neighbourhood.

To cover the costs of life in the convent, the nuns have opened a guesthouse. On specific dates every year they also raise funds by selling their famous Christmas sweets at the entrance.

The success of the low-cost accommodation (previously a women's residence with capacity for fifty university students) has encouraged the congregation to offer lunches, which have become as popular as the Christmas sweets.

The menu is reasonably priced and dishes are home cooked, simple yet filling and prepared lovingly for the convent dining room, which has space for 75 guests.

MIRAVALLE GARDEN VILLA 9
Cuesta del Caldero, 21

The Granada descendants of Montezuma II, emperor of Mexico

There are approximately 350 descendants of the Aztec emperor Montezuma II of Mexico living in Granada today. This imperial bloodline mixed with Spanish nobility is celebrated in the façade of the Miravalle garden villa.

Around the fountain it is still possible to see the Miravalle crown and crest, which bear witness to this ancient Aztec lineage.

It was, in fact, the emperor's oldest daughter who started the noble line that remains in Granada. Isabel Montezuma was married more than once to various Spaniards in the service of the *conquistador* Hernán Cortés.

She and her children maintained their status as descendants of a royal line and were awarded many sinecures and noble titles.

For centuries the Miravalle family were compensated for the loss of their properties with "Montezuma's pensions" (see opposite), established by Carlos V and continued by subsequent Spanish kings and Mexican presidents until the 20th century.

The countess of Granada has publically recognised her Aztec heritage, which today merely brings occasional visits from distant Mexican relatives wishing to pay their respects.

MONTEZUMA'S "AUSTRIAN" CREST

Due to various vicissitudes of history, the crest of quetzal plumes, which served as the crown of Montezuma II, can now be found in the Ethnological Museum of Vienna. Hernán Cortés sent the colourful crest, along with 158 other items, to King Carlos I of Spain when he returned from Mexico. After finding its way into the possession of the monarch's nephew, the Archduke Ferdinand of Hapsburg, who kept it in Ambras castle in the Tyrol, it was later donated to the Ethnographical Museum of Vienna during the Second World War, together with other pre-Hispanic objects.

MONTEZUMA'S PENSION

All descendants of Montezuma II hold a hypothetical right to receive a share of Montezuma's pensions, established in the 16th century to support the descendants of Isabel Montezuma Tecuichpo Ixcaxochitzin.

The amount was established in relation to the land value of areas of the ancient city of Mexico and the part of the city known today as the "countess" neighbourhood.

The dynastic pension was set at 5,258,090 gold pesos per annum, equivalent to 1,480 grams of pure gold (270,622.73 Spanish ounces). This quantity today would be equivalent to 102,209 euros per annum.

The payment was made every year by the Spanish monarchs and taken over by the Mexican government until 1934, when the president of the day, Lázaro Cárdenas, decided to put an end to this colonial right.

THE AZTEC INHERITANCE OF MIRAVALLE

María del Carmen Enríquez de Luna y del Mazo was the twelfth countess of Miravalle, a title created in 1690 for her ancestor Alonso Dávalos Bracamonte. Until her recent death, the countess lived in the centre of modern Granada. María del Carmen was head of the 15th generation of descendants of Isabel Tecuichpo, daughter of Montezuma II, Cuitláhuac and Cuauhtémoc, the last Aztec emperors. Two lines of descendants of Montezuma II lived side by side in Granada. The Miravalle lived in the Cuesta del Caidero palace where their heraldic crown can be seen on the facade. The other Aztec line, descendants of don Pedro Tesifón of Montezuma, the great-grandson in the male line of the Aztec emperor who died in 1639, went to live in La Peza, a village near Granada.

Pedro Tesifón was named Viscount of Llucán, Lord of Tula and Count of Montezuma in 1622. The title of Grandee of Spain was granted to the seventh count, Jerónimo de Oca Montezuma, on 15 December 1265. In 1865, this title was further elevated to Duchy of Montezuma de Tultengo for Antonio Marcilla de Teruel Montezuma y Navarro, thirteenth Count of Montezuma and Marquis of Tenebrón. However, in 1864, the title of Marquis of Montezuma was created and granted to Alonso Holgado y Montezuma, Maestrante of Ronda.

REMAINS OF HYDRAULIC MILLS

Houses of Ángel Ganivet and the Marquis de Rivas
Centre for Ethnological Research
Cuesta de los Molinos, s/n
• Tel: 958 220 157
• Open: 8am-2pm
• Visits organised through the regional government of Granada

> *A medieval mill in the homes of Ángel Ganivet and the Marquis de Rivas*

The Cuesta de los Molinos, running perpendicular to Paseo del Salón, takes its name from the hydraulic mills powered by water transported from the Gorda del Genil reservoir, built by Ahmed ben Jalaf. The mills produced flour and water, but only two remain: the Ángel Ganivet and the Marquis de Rivas. Both have now been carefully restored.

The writer Ángel Ganivet lived in the more famous of the two mills from 1875 until he moved to Madrid at the end of the 1880s. Today, one storey is home to the Centre for Ethnological Research.

Here, one can listen to water running from the underground reservoir beneath the five half-barrel vaults, below which the hydraulic wheels of the ancient mill were located.

A short distance from the Ángel Ganivet, we find the mill home of the Marquis of Rivas, recently restored due to its archaeological importance as one of the few medieval flour mills still working in the 1970s.

This house contains the best maintained architectural elements of an industry of such importance that it gave its name to this part of the neighbourhood.

ÁNGEL GANIVET OR THE TRAGIC WRITER OF GRANADA

Ángel Ganivet García (1865-1898) was one of the most significant writers of the Spanish 19th century and is considered a precursor to the Generation of 98.

Born into a family of millers, he worked in this field until the age of 14. His father died when Ángel was only nine years old. He studied law, philosophy and the humanities, completing his doctorate in Madrid with a thesis on Sanskrit. He found his first job as a librarian and participated actively in the capital's literary life, forging friendships with intellectuals such as Miguel de Unamuno. In 1892 he entered the diplomatic corps and spent four years in Antwerp (Belgium) as vice-consul. His next posting was Helsingfors (Finland), where, after two years of intense writing, he moved to Riga (Latvia) in 1897. Here, he suffered from a serious spiritual crisis, leading to his suicide by drowning in the Dvina River.

His most important works include *Granada the beautiful* (1896) and *Finnish letters* (1896), collections of essays such as *Contemporary Spanish Philosophy* (1889) and *Spanish Ideas* (1898), and *The Sculptor of the Soul* (1898), a play.

ALBAICÍN & SACROMONTE

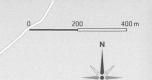

SACROMONTE

Abadía
del Sacromonte

C. Siete Cuestas

Camino del Sacromonte

Camino de Beas

Río Darro

nes
del
alife

MOZARABITE GRAFFITI IN ALBAICÍN ❶

Albaicín walls
• San Martín, 1G

Graffiti from the past

On the Nasrid walls which surround the Albaicín, near Don Gonzalo and the Saint Lawrence Gate, one can see drawings of crosses, keys, horses, deer, anthropomorphic figures and other symbols such as the star of Solomon or the hand of Fatima, inscriptions in Latin or Arabic or diagrams of castles sculpted in the wall. These were left by the Mozarabite Christians under Muslim domination who worked on the construction of the walls of Granada and wanted to express their rebelliousness with drawings or graffiti. It is not surprising that some of the inscriptions on the walls were in Spanish, a linguistic expression of insurgency against the language of their slave masters.

This practice dates back to the Nasrid period (13th to 15th centuries). The Mozarabites were a Christian community tolerated by the Muslim leaders. However, they were obliged to undertake these difficult works as a freedom payment for slaves, according to research by members of the Artistic Centre who made this discovery in 1886 and 1887.

The Mozarabites residing in Granada were descendants of slaves belonging to military commanders who would sell them publically at slave markets in the city to be used as labourers or servants, undertaking the most humble tasks until they could secure their freedom. Many remained in the city once they had obtained their freedom.

The success and rapid expansion of the Muslim domination throughout Europe and the Middle East was due to its particular form of domination. Unlike other cultures, in particular Christian culture, Arabs held onto political power, exercised in the Arabic language, which had to be understood to a high degree in order to work in government. However, the traditions, rites and organisation of the subjugated peoples were tolerated, as long as they paid their taxes.

The city's second defensive wall extended the original perimeter of the Ziri wall that encircled the primitive city in the original nucleus of the Albaicín. The rapid growth of Granada, due to the arrival of inhabitants of other areas conquered by the Christian army, caused the city to reach the impressive number (for that period) of 50,000 inhabitants. In order to expand the city during the medieval period, a second wall was built that reached to Saint Michael on High. It is not surprising that the governors used all the labour available to build and maintain this wall.

OTHER GRAFFITI

In Granada, one can see other graffiti near the Saint Lawrence Gate, inside the Gate of Fajalauza, near the Hermitage of Saint Michael on High and in the Throne Room of the Alhambra.

Granada is not unusual; similar drawings have been found in the excavations of the Medina Azahara in Cordoba.

THE SAINT LAWRENCE GATE

Saint Anthony Hill (behind the church of Saint Christopher)

A sentinel gate

On Saint Anthony Hill (behind the church of Saint Christopher), the Saint Lawrence Gate is a small gate through the exterior wall of the Alhambra that was recovered and identified after being forgotten for many years. Its shape (an irregular rectangle) is unusual - facing towards the north and the west - and the fact that it forms part of a tower makes it a genuine example of an Arab gate, different from any previous examples of the genre. Moreover, it is one of the city's most delightful cultural treasures.

The date of its construction was probably at the end of the 14th century or beginning of the 15th century, under the mandate of Yusuf I and after the Ziri wall, of which it is an integral part.

Since it was re-discovered in 1983, it is believed that its opening and small size were due to the lack of access to Albaicín between the Fajalauza and Elvira gate, which is to say, along almost one and a half kilometres of defensive walls.

The gate is difficult to find; one must climb beyond the Church of Saint Christopher as far as the Fajalauza ceramics factory and then take the road to the left (Saint Anthony Hill). The gate is at the rear of the Church of Saint Christopher, in the area known as Don Gonzalo.

GRAS Y GRANOLLERS MUSEUM ❸

Together with the Daughters of Christ King Teaching Institute
Callejón de la Alberzana, 1
• Tel: 958 291 806
• www.cescristorey.com
• E-mail: cescristorey@cescnstorey.com
• Visit by appointment, arranged with Sister Carmen María Domínguez
• Entry free

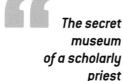

The secret museum of a scholarly priest

In 1993, in commemoration of the 75th anniversary of his death, in his house in Albaicín, where he lived until his death, a small and unknown museum was opened, displaying, among other items, his desk, his reclining chair and many of Father José's personal objects.

An educator, journalist and writer above all, José Gras y Granollers established the Daughters of Christ the King religious order. The nuns from the neighbouring college offer guided tours of the museum, recounting the most important moments of the life of this man of faith.

In the two rooms that comprise this space, one can appreciate the atmosphere in which Gras y Granollers worked and studied. In 1994, his Christian virtues were recognised as heroic through a decree by the Church.

After being ordained as a priest in Barcelona and undertaking various ecclesiastical roles – professor of Theology in Tarragona, assistant rector in Barcelona, teacher in Madrid and Ecija (Seville) – he arrived in Granada as canon of the Sacromonte Abbey. He taught "History of the Church" in the upper seminary at the Abbey and eventually became abbot, before creating

the Academia and Court of Christ association and the magazine *El bien*, which he edited for more than fifty years.

The museum holds many works by the editor of such publications as Barcelona's *Catholic Spain*, Madrid's *Regeneration, Soldier of Christ* (1865), *Europe and its progress with the Church and its dogmas* (1863), *Church and Revolution* (1869), *The Court of the King of Heaven* (1870), *The Saviour of the peoples* (1872), and *The Daughters of Christ, social apostolate for women* (1885).

The silent museum keeps alive the memory of this Catalan who made Granada his home and showcases the dedication of José Gras y Granollers: priest, theologian, Catholic writer and journalist.

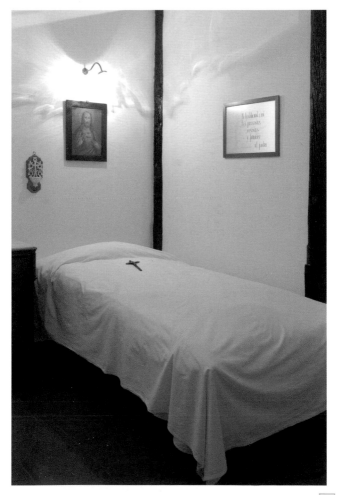

FRAGMENT OF MODERN WALL IN THE CLOSURE OF THE ZIRÍ WALL

④

Hill of Saint Michael on High

> *A bit of modernity in the medieval city walls*

In order to find the fragment of modern wall that the architect Antonio Jiménez Torrecillas designed for the Polvorín route to the isolated hermitage of Saint Michael on High, follow the route of stone along the length of the wall. It has been described as "modern rubbish" and "an ostentatious display of contemporary architecture". The closure of the ancient Ziri wall of Granada in the zenith of the Albaicín, in one of its most rural and untamed areas, does not leave anyone indifferent. Locals and tourists alike are keen to experience or observe the opening used by locals to cross the wall.

Since the beginning of the restoration of the Ziri wall in 2005, there has been much discussion regarding the strange placement of the bricks, which leave space for light to pass through. There have been many complaints about the narrow short-cut through the wall. This segment of contemporary architecture received critical acclaim but was not at all appreciated by the people of Granada.

Antonio Jiménez Torrecilla was the artifice of this contemporary display that attempts to fill a break of approximatcly 40 metres along the Arab wall caused by a 19th-century earthquake. Prizes and references in the most important books of modern architecture were insufficient to stop the Town Hall of Granada blocking the work just as it was coming to completion, insisting on its demolition then requiring a more functional reconstruction, forcing the architect to make a simple opening in one of the lateral walls so that the neighbours could pass through, which had been their request.

THE HERMITAGE OF SAINT CECIL ⑤

Callejón de San Cecil

> **A chapel in the city walls**

The Callejón de San Cecil is home to part of the Arch de las Pesas, where the secluded chapel of Saint Cecil, patron of Granada, is found within a section of the earlier Arab wall. No one can access the interior because it was built as a small altar for thanksgiving in the year 1752. However, from the exterior one can clearly observe a stone image of the saint and martyr, represented as bishop of Ilíberis, who holds the symbolic pomegranate fruit in his hands.

The hermitage was erected by the new Christian residents of the city in order to commemorate the site where, according to popular legend, Saint Cecil was imprisoned with his eleven companions in suffering in the first century AD, shortly before being burnt alive in the caves of Sacromonte (see opposite).

The small chapel is enclosed between the remains of two towers that date from the tenth and eleventh centuries, vestiges forming part of the legendary Granado Castle (*Hizna Román*). The interior of the fortress probably holds a pomegranate tree. According to some scholars, this could be the origin of the city's name.

Granado Castle was protected by the *Bab Qastar* gate, later closed by the Almoravids, according to popular legend. The superstitious believe that this gate served as the entrance for invaders who came to overthrow the power of the Almoravids.

The position of the chapel was chosen carefully as this site is very significant in the history of the city. It is dedicated to the memory of the saint who gave his life to evangelize a people still subjugated to Roman laws.

SAINT CECIL, AN EVANGELISING SAINT

Saint Cecil is considered the first bishop of Ilíberis (Roman Granada) and was one of the "seven preachers", together with Torquatus, Secundius, Indaletius, Ctesiphon, Euphrasius and Hesychius, sent to Boeotia (the name of the Iberian Peninsula during the Roman Empire) by Saint Peter and Saint Paul to proselytise the Gospel of Jesus.

According to oral tradition, we know the story of his trial for treason against the Emperor Nero of Rome. It is believed that after being tortured he was burnt alive to set an example to his followers. After the arrival of King Ferdinand and Queen Isabella, numerous early martyrs, such as Saint Cecil, were venerated locally. Nonetheless, details of his imprisonment in Hizna Román castle cannot be found in any chronicle of the period.

Often mixed with legend, the story of his life has been kept alive over centuries and he is still remembered fondly in Granada. Every year, on the first day of February, there is a pilgrimage to visit the catacombs of Sacromonte Abbey where the patron saint of the city is thought to have been martyred.

THE KING'S CISTERN A N D GARDEN VILLA ❻

Placeta Cristo de las Azucenas
- Tel: 958 200 030
- http://fundacionaguagranada.es/
- Open: Mon-Fri
- Guided tour at 12 noon (groups must reserve by phone)
- Entry free

The culture of water

The King's Cistern, located in the basement of the garden villa of the same name (now beautifully restored), is the largest cistern of the Albaicín and a treasure of Granada's architectural heritage. The provision of water in the Albaicín district is a fine example of civil engineering; the King's Cistern is outstanding.

In this enormous subterranean space, featuring arcades and pillars illuminated by overhead sky lights, one can truly appreciate the fine hydraulic systems of the Arabs, who rightfully considered Granada to be a paradise city.

More than 300 cubic meters of capacity is divided into four sections fed by water from one of the five lines taking water to *Garnatha* (the Arab name for Granada) from its source at Fuente Grande, in the nearby Huétor Sierra, where the Aynadamar water channel first rises.

Small entrance and exit spouts at each end of the room provide evidence of the water's route through this enormous, cool subterranean space, ensuring health and hygiene and providing water to the lower part of the Albaicín neighbourhood.

The villa built over this cistern has been restored on several occasions since the 16th century and holds interesting remains of Nasrid architecture. Today, it is also the site of the Granada Water Visitor Centre, created by the AquaGranada Foundation.

THE ALBAICÍN WATER ROUTE AT A GLANCE

Don't miss the opportunity to visit the enormous scale model of the city to see how water was provided to the inhabitants. Tiny lights indicate the routes of the different water channels through the neighbourhood. At a glance it is possible to see how the medieval city was able to enjoy running water in houses, public baths and plazas while, in the rest of Europe, people had to travel long distances carrying buckets to obtain water for their daily needs.

PALACE OF THE MARQUIS DEL CENETE ❼

Tifia, 28
- Telephone Homees del Pilar: 958 278 036
- Tel: 657 406 720 - 696 849 063
- www.granadaconventual.com
- Group visits organised by Granada Conventual
- Groups of 10+ with advance reservation only
- Guided tour: price tbc

> ### The unknown palace of Granada's last king

This is the one site in Granada where the memory of Boabdil (see opposite) is best preserved. In the relatively unknown palace of the Marquis del Cenete, which today is a school, Boabdil was proclaimed king of Granada in 1487.

Muley Hassan was the nephew of Zagal, the eternal pretender to the throne. Hassan spent his time surrounded by orchards and gardens that still remain today.

During the last days of the Ándalus, the kingdom of Granada was like a swarm of bees so Boabdil sought refuge in this palace, close to his mother who lived in the palace of Dar Al-Horra, during the civil wars between him and his uncle, the prince of Almería.

The original architecture of the palace, still visible in the central patio with a pool and column of Nasrid design, from which various rooms opened off, remained intact until the extensive renovations of the 17th century, which added some portico covered walks around the patio with little aesthetic value.

Following the Reconquista, this simple and charming palace fell into the hands of the Marquis del Cenete, Rodrigo de Mendoza, and was later passed on to one of the principle nobles of the city, José de la Calle y Heredia, a captain of Philip IV, who converted it into a hospital for the poor, dedicated to the Virgin of Pilar. Nuns operated the hospital, which later became an orphanage for girls until 1980 when it was remodelled as a college and concert hall.

BOABDIL, THE UNFORTUNATE KING

Abu Abdallah Muhammad (Granada, 1459 - Fez, 1533) was known as King Muhammad XII of the Nasrid dynasty, although Christians called him Boabdil or Little Boabdil (to differentiate him from his ancestors) as they were unable to pronounce his name correctly. He was also known as Al-Zugaibi, "the Unfortunate". His reign marked the decline of the kingdom of Granada. Various internal struggles, as well as the pressure exercised by the Christian kingdoms, finally conquered him. Muhammad was born in the Alhambra and left Granada on a cold 2 January 1492, for exile in North Africa. He began his public life fighting against his father in Guadix in 1482, supported by *abencerrajes* and by his mother, who installed him on the throne. Constantly battling against his uncle, his father and Christian troops, he was taken prisoner by King Ferdinand and Queen Isabella during the Battle of Lucena. In order to obtain his freedom, he was forced to grant his enemies the lands of Almería dominated by his uncle Zagal, which would eventually spell the end of his kingdom by allowing the Christian troops to advance.

Granada was encircled and its people were exhausted by the siege. Muhammad negotiated some advantageous terms with King Ferdinand and Queen Isabella to ensure that the culture of his people would be honoured in the city, before leaving for exile in Laujar de Andarax then moving on to Fez in Morocco, where he died in 1533.

GARDEN VILLA OF THE CYPRESS TREES ❽

Hill of San Gregorio, 5
• Tel: 958 226 089
• Group visits on request

In the shade of the cypress trees

This is probably the most majestic garden villa in Granada. Over the centuries, it has maintained the original spirit of the villas in Albaicín.

Home to the Spanish diplomat Fernández-Fábregas, it remained a private dwelling even when he became ambassador in Poland. The immense gardens and breathtaking views of the Alhambra make it one of the best viewpoints in Albaicín, or indeed all of modern Granada, allowing one to contemplate the life of the city.

The villa's name is easy to understand due to the large garden surmounted by a pool which, facing towards the Alhambra, seems to indicate the way through the various levels of the estate. Pomegranate trees alternate with lemon trees and persimmons; ivy crawls up the walls mixed with sweet flowering jasmine.

As it is lived in and carefully maintained in every detail by housekeepers and two gardeners, this small palace has not lost the feeling of a home awaiting the return of its residents. Photographs of the family look down from bookcases; lounge chairs anticipate hot days on the glazed porch; the beds are ancient, high and soft; ornate columns support the hanging balcony of the interior patio.

Despite stunning exterior views, inviting contemplation of the surrounding area, the villa is an introspective space, in which we find the room where García Lorca would meet for long afternoons of conversation with his Rinconcillo *tertulia*, in Granada, together with Melchor Soulgro and others, who sadly had to say goodbye when they moved to the modern city of Madrid.

Numerous salons and reception rooms, bedrooms and dressing rooms are decorated in soft, pastel colours. Nothing is out of place. Furnishings appear to live naturally in every space, as if they had been given the freedom to seek harmony.

CHESS IN THE ANDALUS ARAB BATHS ❾

Santa Ana, 1G
- Tel: 958 229 978 - 902 333 334 • www.ajadrezenelagua.com
- Competition in November
- Registration: granada@ajadrezenelagua.com
- Reservations for the baths. granada@hammanalandalus.com

A chess tournament in the water

During the month of November, the Arab baths in Calle Santa Ana, located just below the Tower of the Vela, offer the unique opportunity to play a game of chess submerged in warm waters under a gentle light, as is also traditional in the popular baths in Budapest.

Competitors are surrounded by the heat and steam of the baths, with half their body in the water. Forty players enter the competition to reach the final. Each game has to be less than 15 minutes and follows the established rules of the International Chess Federation (FIDE). The winner receives a trophy but all participants have the right to a celebratory massage.

The Arab baths of Granada were the first establishment of this type to open in the 1990s and they have expanded since then due to their popularity; there are now similar baths in Cordoba, Madrid, and Malaga.

NEARBY

ARAB BATHS DEL BAÑUELO

Carrera del Darro, 31
- Tel: 958 229 738
- Open: Mon-Sun 10am-2:30pm and 5pm-9pm

A few metres from the Santa Ana baths, across the first bridge over the Darro River, we can see some original Arab baths known as the Bañuelo (or Hernando de Zafra). Located behind a private home, here we find some perfectly conserved archaeological remains of the public baths in the lower part of the Albaicín de los Axares, dating from the 11th century.

THE *COBERTIZO* OF THE CARMEN DEL COBERTIZO HOTEL

⑩

Bajo Albaicín
Cobertizo de Santa Inés, 8
• Tel: 958 227 552
• Open: 8am-10pm
• www.carmendelcobertizo.es

> **The oldest cobertizo in all of eastern Andalusia**

A *cobertizo* can be defined as "an upper passage uniting two buildings separated by a street". This architectural curiosity gives a name and an identity to a boutique hotel, the *Carmen del cobertizo,* which has just five rooms.

In this corner of the lower Albaicín, not only can one see a perfect example of a *cobertizo*, typical of Arab and Andalusian architecture, but also the oldest one in all of eastern Andalusia, dating from the 14th century.

Hidden and with access from a cul-de-sac, the hotel takes its name from one of the few *cobertizos* of the Arab period that remain standing in Granada, a type of construction that was almost totally abolished when their construction was outlawed by King Ferdinand and Queen Isabella in order to avoid uprisings by Moors living in the Albaicín.

On this site, the silence is broken only by the sound of running water. A fountain burbles constantly at the centre of a patio with columns, acting as the central point of the residence, a small palace in Renaissance style, built in the 16th century over some 11th-century Arab remains.

On the second floor, the five rooms open on to the central light from the skylights, a modern addition which has made it possible to make the patio of this residence into another room of the house.

The most ancient elements, such as the cistern, have been renovated and today are enjoyed by residents as archaeological exhibits.

THE FIVE *COBERTIZOS* REMAINING IN THE CITY

Of the hundreds which were once found among its streets, only five *cobertizos* remain throughout the city. As well as the *cobertizo* of the hotel, we can see two more in the lower Albaicín: one in calle San Juan de los Reyes, just where it crosses Chapiz hill; the other where calle Gloria crosses Carrera del Darro.

Others are located in Pasaje de Santo Domingo in Realejo and in the Alcaicería, the ancient Arab market at Plaza de Bibrambla.

THE CLOSED WINDOW OF THE CASTRIL MANSION

11

Carrera del Darro, 41-43
• Visible from the exterior

The legend of the walled-up daughter

Above the blind balcony of the Castril Mansion, oddly located just in the corner, the inscription "Waiting for her in heaven" recalls the obscure legend of the daughter of don Hernando de Zafra, third marquis of Castril, who was supposedly imprisoned by her own father to impede her marriage.

According to most of the versions of this sad story, the lord of the manor found his daughter Elvira in a compromising position with Alphonse de Quintanilla, a member of a family who were enemies of the Zafras. The lovers had maintained their secret love affair with the assistance of Father Anthony, the family chaplain.

In revenge for this offence, don Hernando ordered that the intruder be hung from the balcony of that very room. As his daughter begged her father for mercy and implored for divine justice, the Lord of Castril spat furiously, "He will be hung, and he can wait for her in heaven".

After he had executed this horrific punishment, he was still filled with vengeance and imprisoned his daughter in her room, sealing the doors and windows. He then ordered that the cruel words "Waiting for her in heaven" be sculpted on the wall as a warning to dissuade others who might try to stain the family's honour.

However, according to legend, heaven took its revenge against this cruel and inflexible father. His desolate daughter Elvira committed suicide in the room that had become her prison.

Moreover, her father was never to find peace in life or death. On the day he died, when the funeral cortege was in the street, heavy rain fell in Granada and the Darro River burst its banks, causing the corpse to fall into the street and be carried away, so that the vengeful third lord of Castril never received a Christian burial.

Originally, the de Zafra mansion was a Nasrid palace close to the *Maristán* (Hospital), which, like many other buildings, was taken over by a Christian family and given to don Hernando de Zafra, one of the protagonists of the Spanish *Reconquista*.

From 1527, together with other homes nearby, it became part of the convent of the Dominican nuns of Saint Catherine of Siena. The city purchased the villa in 1946 then made some transformations that did not substantially change its original design. Today it is home to the archaeological museum, which is soon to re-open following a period of renovation.

The rooms are distributed around a rectangular patio with a pool and marble fountain at its centre. The second floor was built later. Although it has been in continuous use since its construction, it remains in a good state of conservation and some Arab decorations and inscriptions have survived.

GUEST HOUSE OF THE ROYAL BERNARDINES ⓬

Convent of Saint Bernard
Calle Gloria, 1 (entrance to the guest house from calle Gloria, 2)
• Tel: 958 227 892
• www.conventsanbernardodegranada.com
• Full board: less than 30 €
• Daily meal plan available for non-residents

*The
mysticism
of silence*

Just a few steps from the bustling city centre, in one of the little streets of the lower Albaicín, we find the Convent of Saint Bernard, which gives access to the monastic guest house of the Convent of the Royal Bernardines, where visitors can stay for as long as they wish to share their life of contemplation and service.

These Cistercian nuns belong to one of the strictest orders of monastic life. Although it is not obligatory, one can follow the rhythms of monastic life for a few days, in order to understand how they live throughout the year: the bell rings at 4:30am for the first prayers, as set out by Saint Benedict (480-547) in his rule, then prayers are said throughout the day according to the monastic hours, following a programme of study and work, in a simple and humble manner.

The nuns and novices who live in the convent, no more than a dozen, share the spirit of the Cistercian congregation of Saint Bernard with their guests. However, the only nun who is in contact with the guests is the guest mistress who always speaks quietly out of respect for the life of the convent.

From a balcony in the dining room of the guest house one can see the large

chapel next to the convent, a superb, delicate construction built in 1683 beside the house owned many centuries ago by María de la Torre Esparza.

The guest house comprises seven rooms, two of which are doubles, decorated in an austere style, where silence always reigns. There is space for a maximum of 20 guests. The order was established in 1125 at the abbey of Tart-l'Abbaye (Burgundy, France) and, according to the 2005 census, there are still 164 Cistercian convents worldwide, with 997 nuns.

GLORIOUS FLAVOURS
The sisters are wonderful cooks and make exquisite creams, pastries, fruit jams, Bethlehem cheese and biscuits that one can purchase at the entrance.

SCULPTURE OF APPERLEY THE PAINTER

Placeta de la Gloria

The "English gypsy"

Many artists, once they discover the Albaicín, never leave. This was the case of the English painter Apperley, an aristocratic artist who made his home in a garden villa in Granada.

He is remembered by a small sculpture erected in one of the most charming plazas of the Albaicín district, located in the neighbourhood overlooking the Darro River.

The statue was one of the last works to be completed by the sculptor Mariano Benlliure, who also created the statue of Christopher Columbus in the city centre. It has pride of place in placeta de la Gloria (or Placeta de Apperley), a space created in 2011 from an urban wasteland. The small but very detailed bronze depicts the painter (also known as the "English gypsy") at the height of his creative powers.

Today, the plaza is one of the most charming in this delightful neighbourhood. There is no traffic, there are no tourists, only a few neighbours passing through or the occasional couple seeking a quiet, romantic moment alone in this hidden location. There are a few hedges, flower beds and benches as well as a fence to protect the small sculpture of the painter.

GEORGE APPERLEY

George Owen Wynne Apperley was born in 1884 on the Isle of Wight to an aristocratic Welsh family of soldiers and received a traditional Victorian education. He studied art at the Herkomer Academy then travelled to Italy in 1904, where he first discovered the soft light of the Mediterranean.

At the age of just 20, his works were admired at the annual show at the Royal Academy in London, and in 1916 he moved to Granada, where he specialised in female portraiture. His muse was Enriqueta Contreras, with whom he fell in love. They had two sons, Jorge and Enrique.

He eschewed artistic movements and trends and defended traditional realism. He befriended local painters in Granada such as Soria Aedo, Rodríguez Acosta, López Mosque and Morcillo, whom he would invite to his garden villa at the Saint Nicholas viewpoint, known locally as the "Carmen de Apperley".

In 1945 he was honoured by Alphonse X the Wise and made an Honourable Member of the San Telmo Royal Academy of Fine Arts (Malaga). Due to his openly conservative attitudes, his home was bombed during the difficult years of the Second Republic. For this reason, he moved with his family to Tangiers (Morocco) where he died of a stroke in 1960.

"APPERLIE" PASTRIES

At the López Mosque bakery in Granada, owned by the family of the great impressionist painter José María López Mosque, Federico García Lorca named some sweets filled with strawberry jam as "Apperlies" as they were the painter's favourites.

Indeed, one day when the artist was ill, he sent a servant to purchase "the pastry that Mr. Apperley buys every day", showing them a drawing by the painter himself.

THE "PICHINA" CHAPEL

Carmen de los Patos (Mirador de Morayma Restaurant)
Pianista García Carrillo, 2
• Tel: 958 228 290
• www.miradordemorayma.com
• Open: 1:30pm-11:20 pm, closed Sunday evenings and every Sunday in July and August

Eroticism on the wall

I n the 1970s, a group of art students in Granada would meet together and paint saucy frescoes on the walls of the Carmen de los Patos, ironically referred to as the "pichina" chapel ("picha" is the term for the male member in the slang used in Granada).

As the walls were as white as sheets, the artists decided to give free reign to their creative imagination. The majority of the artists were men and phallic symbols, some of extraordinary proportions, became a dominant motif in all the frescos.

Mariano Cruz, owner of the building and of the Mirador de Morayma restaurant, allowed the artists to meet in the wine cellar of his home during the Franco dictatorship.

Protected by the guise of innocuous gastronomy, artists, writers and bohemians could give free reign to their ideas and expressions. Rafael Guillén, winner of the National Poetry Prize, the writer Francisco Izquierdo and the sculptor Cayetano Aníbal were some of the regulars at these sparkling occasions, during which good food and wine encouraged the exchange of ideas and opinions.

Meetings are still held from time to time in the more comfortable setting of the actual restaurant. Below, the wine cellar holds many bottles as well as cherished memories of those long nights of wine and culture.

VICTORIA GARDEN VILLA ⑮

Cuesta del Chapiz, 9
• Tel: 958 223 122
• Open: Every day 10am-10pm • Entry free

The university's garden villa

Victoria garden villa is the special site where professors invited to give lectures or participate in short research projects at the University of Granada can enjoy the luxury of contemplating the view of the Alhambra every day when they wake.

The building is a typical example of Arab architecture; the garden is paradigm of the terraced gardens with floral diversity, and especially an impressive creeper, which has grown over the centuries to incredible dimensions.

Currently, this garden villa is used principally as a residence for visiting professors since it was purchased by the University of Granada in 1945. However, its current design dates from the end of the 19th century when part of the early Convent of the Victoria was joined to the Carmen Olivarillo-Percal.

GRANADA, THE CITY OF THE GARDEN VILLAS

Granada is known as the city of the garden villas (*ciudad de los carmenes*) as the garden villa has been the most typical type of local home since Arab times. More than a building, it represents a lifestyle and a way of understanding that still remains today due to the zeal of the few remaining owners of these villas, which are luxurious and austere at the same time. The word *carmen* comes from the Arabic *karm*, meaning "vineyard" or "vine".

The concept has been defined as a "Granada estate, with orchard and garden" or as a "recreational estate which is also functional". The *carmen* has three principal elements: an extensive residence with a tower, a garden and a wall which separates it from the street to maintain the privacy and intimacy of the home, according to Muslim philosophy.

The villas, built on sloping ground, were originally modest brick constructions using materials such as plaster, whitewash and mosaics – simple materials that create the impression of a wealthy and indeed luxurious home.

The modern garden villa is a baroque construct dating from the early 17th century, after the expulsion of the Moors from the Albaicín. This densely populated neighbourhood turned into an empty ruin in just two years, from 1568 to 1570.

In the 19th century, influenced by orientalists, the educated bourgeoisie rebuilt the ancient garden villas, decorating them with false oriental details. Since then, ownership of a garden villa in the Albaicín is synonymous with wealth and good taste. There are garden villas in the Albaicín neighbourhood and on both sides of the Darro and Genil Rivers, zones where the canalisation of drinking water through aqueducts and cisterns made it possible to build these traditional homes. Other neighbourhoods such as Antequeruela, Realejo and Cuesta de la Churra also have several charming garden villas.

AVE MARÍA SCHOOLS

Cuesta del Chapiz, 20
• Tel: 958 229 456-958 221 460
• http://casamadre.amgr.es/
• Open: Mon-Friday 9am-1pm
• Visit by appointment

> *Father Manjón's innovative didactic pedagogy*

The Ave María schools of Sacromonte are an educational institution established by Father Andrés Manjón y Manjón, a pioneer in the field of pedagogy. The schools were open mainly for the children of Sacromonte, the majority of whom were gypsies; they were taught the catechism and given an elementary education. Given their social marginalisation and the high rate of illiteracy, Manjón designed an innovative educational system based on a child's natural impulse to play as a means to understand their studies. The school area extends for more than a kilometre and a half along the bank of the Darro River and is formed by the unification of eight neighbouring garden villas.

Although nearby caves were converted into classrooms and student residences, classes were also given in the open air. Theory and practice came together in sewing, ironing, washing, cooking, shoe repairs, carpentry and printing workshops. There were also drawing classes offered by the prestigious painters Manuel Gómez-Moreno and la Rocha.

Today, although the cave schools no longer exist, one can make an appointment to visit some exhibits of the unconventional teaching methods, such as the unusual map-pond for teaching geography, historical games and games for learning the planets, charts of numbers and letters or flashcards to make words.

One can also visit the office of Andrés Manjón to see a recreation of his bedroom with his personal effects: coats, boots, the hoods for his law degree and his appointment as canon of Sacromonte, his bed, wash basin and the sheets used as his shroud.

FATHER ANDRÉS MANJÓN Y MANJÓN

Andrés Manjón y Manjón (Sargentes de la Lora, 1846-Granada, 1923), theologian, jurist and teacher, was born into a humble family. He studied philosophy and theology in Burgos.

Later, after being ordained a priest (1886), he graduated in Law in Valladolid. In Madrid he taught at Saint Isadore College, where he discovered his true vocation, teaching. He was made a professor of canon law in Santiago in 1829 then taught at the University of Granada, where he wrote his *Treatise on Canon Law*.

He discovered the neighbourhood of the Sacromonte when he became a canon of the abbey. His intense pedagogical work at the Ave María schools led to a worldwide teaching revolution.

HERMITAGE OF CHRIST OF THE POLE

Camino del Sacromonte, 47

The gypsy Christ

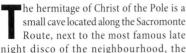

The hermitage of Christ of the Pole is a small cave located along the Sacromonte Route, next to the most famous late night disco of the neighbourhood, the Camborio cave discotheque. The cave features a curious painting known in Sacromonte as "Christ of the Pole", venerated in this area due to its gypsy connotations. The pole (or striped rod) is one of the instruments used in the gypsy harvest festivals. The image is a poorly executed copy as the original, dating from the 17th century, is kept in the home of the owner of the small church.

The representation of Christ on the column, crowned with thorns and with his hands tied, is illuminated day and night by a lantern that also illuminates other paintings on the side walls and the cupula of the little sanctuary, which is always filled with fresh flowers and lit candles.

Various local women take responsibility for the maintenance of the hermitage, ensuring cleaning and security, even though the original painting is now kept elsewhere. In order to see the interior, you will need to wait for one of these women, who visit the site from time to time but without any regular schedule.

The cross, which marked this point of the *vía crucis* of the Sacromonte Route, disappeared years ago. Nonetheless, the hermitage has remained largely ignored by the tourism that has transformed much of the avenue

into a kind of folkloric museum. The church has never received any assistance for its restoration. As throughout the area, there is a lack of interest from the municipal authorities, who have never been able to commit to plans for the overall renovation of this unique Granada neighbourhood. The owners of the hilltop disco have expressed interest in purchasing it as the space would be useful for them to store cases of drinks.

Despite all the blows to progress, the gypsy Christ of the Sacromonte Route remains illuminated and serves as a focal point for the neighbourhood, with a curious mix of devotion and superstition that permeates each corner of this sacred yet untamed site.

SACROMONTE CAVES VISITOR CENTRE AND MUSEUM ⓲

Ravine de los Blacks, Sacromonte
- Tel: 958 215 120
- www.sacromontegranada.com
- info@sacromontegranada.com
- Open: Mon-Sun 10am-8pm (Mar 15 - Oct 14); Mon-Sun 10am-6pm (Oct 15 - Mar 14)
- Admission: 5 €; Groups (15): 3 € per person
- Guided tour of the museum: 5 € per person (groups of 15 minimum)
- Approximate duration of the tour: 1 hour

A cave home

Ten years ago, the Visitor centre and Ethnographical Museum were opened at the Sacromonte caves, a difficult site to access where one can learn about life in the caves, a tradition kept alive in the city of Granada and its province. In this museum one can visit various cave residences, which were inhabited until the middle of the 20th century. Managed by the Vaivén Paradise Association, the museum offers abundant information about this unique lifestyle.

The cave residences were typical of the Sacromonte neighbourhood. They were inhabited by local families taking advantage of a constant temperature of between 18 and 22 degrees and the shelter provided from extreme heat and cold conditions.

The relationship between human and cave is dynamic, allowing inhabitants to carve their way into the mountain if they need more space. Their construction requires waterproof terrain and they consist of several adjoining rooms: the façade with window and gate facing towards the east;

the chimney and the interior patio excavated opposite the gate; the first room and a hallway leading into a large kitchen, the heart and soul of the cave and the matriarch's territory. The bedrooms extend the residence by carving out rooms towards the interior of the mountain. The rooms with the most light were used for working: the men would produce baskets made from reeds or cane while the women embroidered, sewed and knitted.

For many centuries the Sacromonte caves served as a refuge for the marginal population of the city: Moors and later gypsies. In recent decades, with global warming, these residences have been re-discovered, and are constantly being renovated as luxurious homes for artists and foreigners looking for tranquillity with a touch of the exotic.

THE PRINCE OF THE GYPSIES

The patriarch Mariano Fernández, "Chorrojumo" (a nickname taken from the words *chorro*, or filth, and *humo*, smoke), was the incarnation of the

stereotypical image of a 19th-century gypsy.

Chorrojumo gave up work as a blacksmith to walk around the Alhambra, allowing tourists to take photos of him in a gypsy "costume".

He would regale visitors with stories and even sell his own photographs, the most famous being by Ayola. The painter Mariano Fortuny discovered this character, who represented the history of Granada and was depicted on tourist postcards.

Due to the economic success of his initiative, he was able to move away from Sacromonte. However, he succumbed to a heart attack as he walked by the Alhambra, where he had become a human part of the décor. In more than forty years of professional life, he saw off many competitors and no one can dispute his status as prince of the gypsies.

TEA SHOP AT VALPARAISO RAVINE (OR GRANGE OF THE AIR)

19

Valparaiso ravine

I n the upper part of the Valparaiso ravine ravine in Sacromonte, a tea shop displays a bright poster which states "Grange of the air" in reference to the grange once located here. Another poster indicates that this tea room is managed by the "Free University Cultural Centre".

A historic and alternative tea shop

The scholar Antonio Villar Yebra theorised that, in the time of the Moors, this was a hidden hermitage where Jewish *conversos* were baptised.

Below the gentle pines, Ismael, the owner of a cave, began to offer cool drinks to hikers.

Over time, by recycling found materials (tires from cars or lorries, pieces of wood and stone), he installed tables and chairs where visitors can sit today and discover this hidden corner not to be found on any map.

The owner of the residence and tea shop has lived here for 20 years, surrounded by his collection of books and the slight electric light provided by a small solar panel, recently installed.

He lives in the same way as his neighbours in Valparaiso ravine, in caves

along the Sacromonte Route in the direction of the abbey. In many cases, ownership of the caves cannot be traced due to the absence of land ownership registers.

Sometimes the appearance of this "troglodyte avenue" appears different from more conventional neighbourhoods due to the lack of municipal lighting or any public drainage network.

CUTI CISTERN

Valparaiso ravine
Cave always open

The lost cistern

The Cuti fountain is found in one of the paths along the Sacromonte of Granada, which travel through the dusty land of the area where the Sacromonte population has always lived in very rural caves and shacks.

The cistern is found in a remote corner and goes unmentioned in all the guides and catalogues of Granada's fountains. The cave is always open and worth a visit due to its archaeological interest. It lies beyond the Sacromonte Abbey, the Orange ravine and the Black Ravine in an area called Valparaiso, where time seems to have stood still for centuries.

It is very surprising to find this well in the ground, in the middle

of an unnamed path and without any indication of its existence beyond a pointed brick arch marking its entrance. Only the neighbours of the fountain, who use the water from the cistern for their domestic needs, know the bloody history of this natural spring (see opposite).

The function of the cistern is simply to collect the water that filters down from the interior of the mountain until it reaches an impermeable layer of clay. At a depth of about one hundred metres, water drips into the cave's interior and is collected in simple brick pools due to channels carved into the earth.

ESCAPE AND DEATH OF A WARRIOR

A recent police report told the story of the Gaurdia Civil's man hunt in the 1940s to find a legendary anti-Franco warrior who had hidden in the Cuti cistern. According to the document, the rebellious Quero brothers were involved in unbelievable persecutions and were injured in the streets of the city.

In July of 1945, two of the brothers, Francisco and Pedro, were sought by the Guardia Civil. They were involved in a gun battle during which Francisco was shot in the eye. During their escape Pedro broke a leg and his brother Francisco carried him on his shoulder as they made their way into the depths of Sacromonte.

They decided to separate so there would be a greater chance that at least one of them would survive. Pedro made it as far as the Cuti fountain. He hoped to save himself by remaining in his hideout but he was blocked by the enemy who encircled the only exit. Without any way to escape, Pedro shouted that they would have to come in to capture him. Two members of the Guardia Civil tried to access the narrow cistern and were killed as the mouth of the cistern had been armed with 7 kilos of dynamite. Pedro continued to shout and they dared to enter.

When Pedro realised there was no escape, he pretended to hand himself over but requested a final cigarette. One of his sisters-in-law present at the siege took him some tobacco then began to cry. The guards became impatient and ordered him to come out with his hands in the air. In response, they heard a shot and everyone present was paralysed with shock. Pedro Quero's sister-in-law was forced to enter again to collect his lifeless body. Thus he fulfilled the promise made to his brothers than none of them would be taken prisoner.

THE STARS OF DAVID AT SACROMONTE ABBEY ㉑

Camino de Sacromonte, 4
• Tel: 958 221 445
• Open: Tue-Sun 11am-1pm and 4pm-6pm

Not just a Hebrew symbol

To the great surprise of many visitors, Sacromonte Abbey is full of Stars of David, or rather six-pointed hexagrams. They can be seen in the main entrance gate, in the door to the Abbey and in various sites on the external walls. For some, this important symbol has not always been a Jewish symbol. Until the 14th century, it was also an important symbol for Christians and Muslims.

Among the famous lead books (see page 116) to be found in the Abbey, there is one dedicated specifically to the seal of Solomon entitled: *Book of the history of the seal of Solomon. History of the seal of the prophet Solomon, and of David and his mysteries, according to the Virgin Mary*, written by Cecilio Ebnelradi, a disciple of Saint James.

For more information about the symbolism of the Star of David, see following double-page spread.

For more information about the esoteric meaning of the lead books as a possible "fifth Gospel", see page 116.

THE STAR HEXAGRAM: A MAGICAL TALISMAN?

The hexagram – also known as the Star of David or the Shield of David – comprises two interlaced equilateral triangles, one pointing upwards and the other downwards. It symbolises the combination of man's spiritual and human nature.

The six points correspond to the six directions in space (north, south, east and west, together with zenith and nadir) and also refer to the complete universal cycle of the six days of creation (the seventh day being when the Creator rested).

Hence, the hexagram became the symbol of the macrocosm (its six angles of 60° totalling 360°) and of the union between mankind and its creator.

Although present in the synagogue of Capernaum (third century AD), the hexagram does not really make its appearance in rabbinical literature until 1148 – in the *Eshkol Hakofer* written by the Karaite* scholar Judah Ben Elijah. In Chapter 242 its mystical and apotropaic (evil-averting) qualities are described, with the actual words then often being engraved on amulets: "And the names of the seven angels were written on the *mazuzah*: The Everlasting will protect you and this symbol called the Shield of David contains, at the end of the *mezuzah*, the written name of all the angels."

In the thirteenth century the hexagram also became an attribute of one of the seven magic names of Metatron, the angel of the divine presence associated with the archangel Michael (head of the heavenly host and the closest to God the Father).

The identification of Judaism with the Star of David began in the Middle Ages. In 1354 King Karel IV of Bohemia granted the Jewish community of Prague the privilege of putting the symbol on their banner. The Jews embroidered a gold star on a red background to form a standard that became known as the Flag of King David (*Maghen David*) and was adopted as the official symbol of Jewish synagogues. By the nineteenth century, the symbol had spread throughout the Jewish community. Jewish mysticism has it that the origin of the hexagram was directly linked with the flowers that adorn the *menorah***: irises with six petals. For those who believe this origin, the hexagram came directly from the hands of the God of Israel, the six-petal iris not only resembling the Star of David in general form but also being associated with the people of Israel in the *Song of Songs*.

As well as offering protection, the hexagram was believed to have magical powers. This reputation originates in the famous *Clavicula Salomonis* (Key of Solomon), a grimoire (textbook of magic) attributed to Solomon himself but, in all likelihood, produced during the Middle Ages. The anonymous texts probably came from one of the numerous Jewish schools of the Kabbalah that then existed in Europe, for the work is clearly inspired by the teachings of the Talmud and the Jewish faith.

The *Clavicula* contains a collection of thirty-six pentacles (themselves symbols rich in magic and esoteric significance) which were intended to enable communication between the physical world and the different levels of the soul.

There are various versions of the text, in numerous translations, and the content varies between them.

However, most of the surviving texts date from the sixteenth and seventeenth centuries – although there is a Greek translation dating from the fifteenth.

In Tibet and India, the Buddhists and Hindus read this universal symbol of the hexagram in terms of the creator and his creation, while the Brahmins hold it to be the symbol of the god Vishnu.

Originally, the two triangles were in green (upright triangle) and red (inverted triangle). Subsequently, these colours became black and white, the former representing the spirit, the latter the material world. For the Hindus, the upright triangle is associated with Shiva, Vishnu and Brahma (corresponding to the Christian God the Father, Son and Holy Ghost).

The Son (Vishnu) can be seen to always occupy the middle position, being the intercessor between things divine and things earthly.

The hexagram also often appears in the windows and pediments of Christian churches, as a symbolic reference to the universal soul. In this case, that soul is represented by Christ – or, sometimes, by the pair of Christ (upright triangle) and the Virgin (inverted triangle); the result of the interlacing of the two is God the Father Almighty. The hexagram is also found in the mediated form of a lamp with six branches or a six-section rose window.

*qara'im or bnei mikra: "he who follows the Scriptures". Karaism is a branch of Judaism that defends the sole authority of the Hebrew Scripture as the source of divine revelation, thus repudiating oral tradition.
**Menorah – the multibranched candelabra used in the rituals of Judaism. The arms of the seven-branched menorah, one of the oldest symbols of the Jewish faith, represent the seven archangels before the Throne of God: Michael, Gabriel, Samuel, Raphael, Zadkiel, Anael and Kassiel.

THE LEAD BOOKS: THE "FIFTH GOSPEL"?

Considered heretical, apocryphal and an invention of the Moors of Granada at the end of the Middle Ages and early Renaissance, the lead books of Sacromonte, written in Arab and Latin on sheets of lead, remain an enigma. In the 16th century, the "old tower" stood on Mount Valparaiso (where the Sacromonte Abbey stands today on the "sacred mountain" of Granada). It was the ancient minaret of the biggest Nasrid mosque. When it was demolished, a crypt was discovered. Here, Francisco Hernández and Sebastián López of Granada found a lead box on 18 March 1588, the feast of Saint Gabriel (the archangel who dictated the *Koran* to the Prophet Mohammed). The next day was the feast of Saint Joseph, the husband of the Virgin Mary, who is thought to have inspired the lead books dictated to the Muslim mullahs (the saint makes frequent apparitions in the texts). Various other objects were found in the box: a tablet with an image of Jesus wearing "Egyptian" (gypsy) dress, clothing that was forbidden to the Moors of Granada, a cloth belonging to the Virgin Mary and a *pergamen* written in Arabic, Spanish and vulgar Castilian Latin, which is one of the oldest sources for the life of Saint Cecil the martyr, the patron of Granada. The bishop of Granada, don Pedro de Castro, was greatly surprised and pleased by the discovery and insisted that excavations continue. Some circular lead sheets were found bearing writings in Latin and Arabic about saints martyred during the reign of the Emperor Nero. One bears the following title: "Burnt body of san Monthtión, martyred in the time of the Emperor Nero". A notebook was also found with circular lead pages, entitled *De Fundamentum Ecclesiae,* which told of other saints such as Saint Hesychius, a disciple of the Apostle Saint James. The notebook described the martyrdoms that many saints had suffered.

From all the information and relics obtained until 1599, one name stood out: Saint Cecil, one of the mythical Seven Apostolic Men who, according to these texts, had converted to Islam after the Muslim invasion of the Iberian Peninsula.

Although this is historically impossible (Saint Cecil lived in the third century AD and the invasion took place in the eighth century), it has symbolic value. Muslim theology describes the "Seven Wise Men of the Cavern", who are very similar to the Seven Apostolic Men.

However, the most surprising aspect of these writings is their description of a new fifth gospel, written by the Virgin Mary and read throughout the Iberian Peninsula.

This "Fifth Gospel" was of great interest to pilgrims to Santiago de Compostela. The lead books often make reference to Saint James and the Virgin Mary, who is said to have instructed him to travel to the Iberian Peninsula guided by the Archangel Gabriel in order to hide (with the meaning of "hidden wisdom") these lead books in various sites in Granada.

Historically, the Apostle is widely respected in Spain and even venerated by some Muslims. Indeed, the terrible warrior Soulnzor did not touch the cathedral when he attacked Santiago de Compostela in the tenth century because the mortal remains of the patron of the Iberian Peninsula were kept there.

Jews and Arabs were often seen on pilgrimage to Compostela, together with Christians.

The Santiago pilgrimage route was a moment of spiritual growth, offering an opportunity for confession and the remission of sin. Alchemy, cabala and other hermetic wisdom was part of the cultural and spiritual formation of many Christian pilgrims who studied at mosques and synagogues.

The 22 circular sheets of lead, approximately 10cm each, known as the *Lead Books of Sacromonte,* are engraved with hermetic symbols and alchemistic characters in Arabic that some agnostic researchers, unaware of the Arab-Jewish esoteric world, have referred to as the writings of Solomon. In actual fact, these 22 lead books are a final attempt to reconcile Christianity with Islam after the *Reconquista* of Granada in 1492 by King Ferdinand and Queen Isabella.

The new monarchs had promised to respect and maintain the laws and customs of the Arab population, but the promise was ignored by Cardinal Cisneros, who obliged the Moors to convert and prohibited their practices and traditions. This caused an uprising in 1500-1501, and another in 1568 known as the Alpujarra Rebellion, which was harshly repressed. While the Catholic Church sought to Christianise the Moorish community through armed repression, the mosque of Granada sought to Islamise Catholicism culturally through the lead books. Thus in these texts we find a Christian *shahada* or "profession of faith" in preparation for the Muslim *shahada*, which is presented as superior, albeit in a manner that it was hoped Christians could accept. Jesus appears as the symbol of Sanctity and Mohammed as the symbol of Prophecy.

The spirituality expressed in the lead books is the adoration of a Most High God, in the Muslim tradition, slightly influenced by the cult of Christ, as can be seen in one of the books commonly used by members of both religions: the *Kitab al hikam ad Din,* or "Book of the Sentences on the Law". This is a marvellous Islamic and also Christian devotional, containing formulae that constantly recall the essentials of faith in God. It can be read by members of both religions, as its authors specifically intended.

The Islamic veneration of Jesus and of Maria is expressed on several occasions in the lead books according to Muslim tradition, without ever

mentioning God, with the exception of some allusions to the Trinity, which could make such an interpretation possible. However, the most relevant figure of these apocryphal texts (apocryphal meaning "secret" according to its Greek etymology) is Mary the Virgin, also venerated by Islam. Indeed the Koran contains the words "Ave Maria" as pronounced by the archangel Gabriel.

Mary is the principal character of the most beautiful of the lead books, the *Kitab minha as cilha Maryam al Adra*, or "Book of the Virgin Mary's Conversations", a version of the "Book of the Stairway of Mohammed", which is alleged to be one of the sources of inspiration for Dante's *Divine Comedy*. It has the merit of offering the Christian imagination a vision of Paradise and Inferno, which is almost absent in the Bible.

For the Moors of Granada, this vision of Paradise was like a transfiguration of the fields of Granada. The beautiful city, with its four gates, its orchards and the Sacro Monte, was the perfect prototype of Eden.

The lead books of Sacromonte were taken to Madrid in 1631 and then, years later, to Rome for study until in 1682 Pope Innocent XI declared them to be false and heretical, although the relics found with them were declared to be authentic. Fortunately, the Vatican did not destroy these unique works, which were returned to Granada in June 2000 through an initiative of Pope Benedict XVI. Today, one can admire some examples of the 22 lead books in the Sacromonte Abbey Museum.

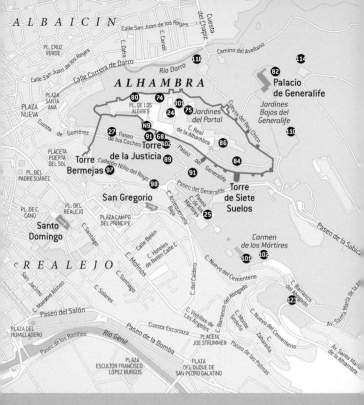

ALHAMBRA

0   200   400 m

N

Parque periurbano Dehesa del Generalife

Cementerio
de San José

Canal de los Franceses Dudar

TUNNEL OF THE SMALL KING ❶

Path descending to the Darro River in front of the building of the Small King
(Centre for Theatrical Art)
Tunnel in the river bank always open

Waterfall below the Alhambra

The tunnel of the Small King starts at the bank of the Darro River and leads towards the centre of the hill of the Alhambra.

It is a subterranean gallery three and a half metres in height where water from the stream flows continuously over the stone floor. Some meters above, it descends parallel to Chinese Hill.

The majority of passers-by fail to notice the tunnel because it is covered by abundant vegetation on the riverbank. The only indication of its presence is the water that rises to ankle height, producing a small lateral waterfall into the river, which tells us that we are at the entrance of the tunnel below the Small King building.

We can hear the sound of falling water in the distance. This is the end of the subterranean tube that channels water from the stream below ground just under the Tower of the Ladies, through a dark tunnel some 100 metres deep. The pool that produces the waterfall from the siphon is very large.

The existence of all these tunnels to the Alhambra from every corner of the city is one of the many legends that add to the romance of the palace on

the red hill.

They were excavated to ensure provisions in case of siege, one of the most commonly used strategies to defend any fortress.

Also, some passages allow visitors to come and go without drawing attention to themselves, which is always important for diplomacy and intrigue.

Much has been said about the tunnels under the Alhambra, although few have visited them.

This is one of the easiest to access. Others, especially those from the Tower of the Ladies or of the Comares Tower, have been closed by the Alhambra authorities.

THE WATER STAIRS
Gardens of the Generalife

> *Federico García Lorca's favourite corner*

Given this name due to the channels of water that run alongside them, the water stairs are a perfect example of the aesthetics of the architectural complex that is the Alhambra. Necessity becomes a virtue.

The staircase was built between the 13th and 15th centuries and today it is almost hidden by the vegetation surrounding what was once the access route to a small oratory situated in the uppermost part of the wall.

This was the favourite corner of Federico García Lorca and Manuel of Falla, who immortalised this atmosphere in his music. The simplicity of the water stairs transforms this hidden corner of the garden into a celestial song, in which it is possible to hear the stream and smell the aroma of the delightful

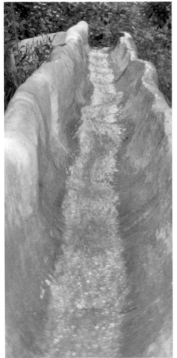

laurel along its route. The water runs along the banisters with a lively sense of fun created by the placement of upside down roof tiles on the lateral walls, thereby channelling the water from the Royal Ditch. The water moves through three pools that form along its route then builds strength in order to re-commence its frolicking, before finally resting in some small circular ponds.

Another subterranean channel creates a small fountain in the centre of each circle, the sound of which is a counterpoint for the overall symphony that invites the soul to play. This construction has provided inspiration to those who, like Lorca and de Falla, have been able to appreciate the sensation of walking up this staircase and enjoying the cool and ingenious system of ablutions prior to prayer, initially Muslim, then Christian and today, simply human.

THE ROYAL DITCH ❸

Generalife Paddock
Access by the Winter Park road (Llano del Perdiz)

The Alhambra's source of life

A channel providing life-giving water demonstrates the complex Arab engineering systems that provide the Alhambra with water for the gardens, orchards, baths, mosques, houses, cisterns, fountains and gardens, as well as drinking water for those within the palace walls.

The intelligent hydraulic system is a marvel for engineers and architects all over the world. It belongs to an initial channel called the Ditch of the Sultan, known today as the Royal Ditch. This large principal channel, some eleven kilometres in length, takes water directly from the Darro River, six kilometres above the urban waterway.

This permanent flow of water begins its sloped journey to the Generalife-Cerro del Sol meadows at an artificial derivation of the river, near the Jésus del Valle *cortijo*, and reaches all the way to the fortress. It provides water to other smaller ditches, such as the Generalife Ditch and the Tercio Ditch, which once fed the now long-gone palaces of Dar Al Arusa and Alixares, as well as St Helen's Castle and several waterwheels placed at various levels to provide water to the Alhambra.

King Al-Ahmar ibn Nasr, founder of the Nasrid dynasty and the sultan of Granada between 1232 and 1273, began the works to open this "river" for the Alhambra. It continues to sustain the living beauty of the complex.

LOS ALBERCONES

Paseo de las Adelfas
- Tel: 958 027 900-958 027 971
- www.alhambra-management.es
- E-mail: information.alhambra.pag@juntadeanadalucia.es
- Visits arranged as part of the annual programme of "Guided visits with specialists of the Alhambra of Granada"
- For more information contact the Alhambra Management

Water, a valuable commodity

Los Albercones is a hydraulic complex situated in the upper part of the Alhambra, above the Generalife, which includes the Tower of the Ladies, various reservoirs and conduits. These reservoirs of water from the Royal Ditch, channelled by a subterranean derivation below the Tower of the Ladies, were vital for the supply and control of water for all of the Alhambra.

Even though this site, with its millions of visitors, relies on the judicious and discreet distribution of water, few know about the network that allows for this constant flow of life. Although it is not part of the usual tourist circuit, los Albercones, which is located further up the Paseo de las Adelfas, is quite visible to those who know where to look.

The network is composed of three levels, each of which has its own reservoir. It was extended in the 19th and 20th centuries, when two other reservoirs were added to those fed by an underground gallery. The channels end in a well below a small tower, the Tower of the Ladies, which was built both to protect it and to house the wheel that took water from the Royal Ditch.

Brick platforms surround the reservoir, as well as a stairway to a terrace and pavillion with a viewpoint overlooking Los Albercónes. All this hydraulic engineering not only includes a canal between the reservoirs, but also a subterranean passage used for maintenance and cleaning.

Medieval travellers were greatly impressed with the Alhambra and its excellent living conditions with luxuries unthinkable in Europe at that time (13th to 15th centuries). There was a densely populated urban area with up to 30,000 people, who, apart from the fountains and the permanently watered gardens, also enjoyed a pool, drinking water and even modern comforts such as toilets with running water, something unthinkable in the "backward" Christian culture of those times.

When the nomad people arrived on the fertile plain criss-crossed by three rivers (the Darro, Beiro and Genil), they understood and enjoyed this resource that was more precious than gold in their homeland.

THE ROUTE AROUND THE ALHAMBRA

Nasrid Palaces of the Alhambra
Real de la Alhambra, s/n
• Tel: 958 027 971
• www.alhambra-patronato.es
• E-mail: alhambra.pag@juntadeanadalucia.es
• Visit included with general admission to the Alhambra during one
month each year as part of the 'Site of the month' programme. Check the
website to find out which month.

How to defend a marvel

The Alhambra parapet walk is a passage along the Alhambra's defensive walls which was used to connect the various parts of the complex, as did a protective moat and the internal path the guards used to gain rapid access to the battlements to defend the palaces.

Built between the 13th and 14th centuries and hidden within the walls of the Alhambra, it is one of the best examples of the monument's defensive nature. It is still under renovation and it can be difficult to follow its path in some areas. Only the section between the Lindraja patio and the Picos Tower is open to visitors.

Together with the Alcazaba, a castle with fortified walls around a small citadel that housed the sultan's guard independently from the rest of the fortress, the parapet walk served to reinforce defences. The walls of the Alhambra were known for their resistance to long attacks or sieges; they were never taken. The last king of Granada preferred to hand over his city rather than see it destroyed, so he carefully negotiated the handover of his kingdom with the provision that the traditions of the local population would be respected, which was the case for half a century.

Large towers were added later, thus shaping the current structure; in time, they were given such beautiful names as the Tower of the Seven Floors or the Tower of the Captive. Below and around the towers, the walk runs parallel along the entire length of the defensive wall, which has survived the passage of time.

THE ENEMY AT HOME

The Alhambra lies on top of Al Sabika Hill, overlooking the city and standing directly opposite the ancient city of *Garnata*, on the other side of the river on the slopes of the Albaicín (which has its own fortress, the Alcazaba Cadima). Before the arrival of the Christian armies, this "distance" between the two led the kings of Granada to fear intrigues and uprisings from their own people. The struggles over the throne between various rival factions within the ruling family of the Alhamar were legendary.

NEARBY

THE SECRET STAIRS TO THE QUEEN'S CHAMBER
Alhambra Woods

The tower known as the Queen's Chamber, which housed the boudoir of Empress Isabella, wife of Charles V, is reached by a steep and winding stairway through part of the Alhambra Woods.

This "secret" stairway, visible from the Partal gardens, was discovered in 1831. It passes through the lower part of the tower and dies out at a landing in the woods.

THE NICHES OF THE ALHAMBRA ⑥

On both sides of the entrance to each room of the palace

Water in the Alhambra

On either side of the arches or doorways to the rooms you'll find a pair of niches directly in the wall. Although visitors to the palace might consider them mere decorations, they have a very specific function. They were used to hold jugs of water so the inhabitants of the Alhambra could quench their thirst as they entered or left each room. Water from the niches was also used for ablution rites (see opposite), a purification process that Muslims carry out before prayer.

Water was a luxury enjoyed in abundance by the descendants of the desert tribes who lived in Granada, as demonstrated by the great number of fountains, reservoirs and moats which made the area so lovely.

THE USE OF WATER IN ISLAMIC ABLUTION RITUALS

For Muslims, water is a fundamental part of the ablution ritual. In this ancient rite, the faithful wash their hands, the instruments of action, and gargle, thus simulating the act of drinking from the fountains of paradise. They wash their forearms, which represent the strength with which the world is built; they aspirate water through their noses, which receive the aroma of the garden; they wet their brow, the source of wisdom; they clean their ears, which represent sound; and finally they wash their legs, which carry them along the path to the divine presence.

VAULTED CRYPT OF CHARLES V

Palace of Charles V (La Alhambra)
Real de la Alhambra, s/n
• Tel: 958 027 900-958 027 971
• www.alhambra-management.es
• E-mail: informacion.alhambra.pag@juntadeanadalucia.es
• Visit included with general admission to the Alhambra during one
month each year as part of the 'Site of the month' programme. Check the
website to find out which month.

*The room
of secrets*

The basement of the Palace of Charles V is home to the crypt or room of secrets, which connects with the Alhambra and other zones of the palace.

The ingenious architect Pedro Machuca had fun designing this room, which, although secluded, is one of the most visited in the palace.

The acoustics are perfect for sharing secrets : if you whisper at one end of the room, your words will be heard clearly at the other end.

This game is known only to a few and can surprise some visitors who walk past one corner and begin to hear voices arriving from somewhere else. Their surprise quickly turns to smiles when they realise that someone is whispering

to the wall at the other side of the octagonal room, speaking into a stone corner, which acts like a sort of medieval telephone or intercom.

PASSAGES BELOW THE PALACE OF CHARLES V

Emperor Charles V ensured that his palace had good communication with the nearby Nasrid Palaces by building internal underground passages. The construction of these connecting passages involved the demolition of some parts of the Nasrid Palaces, but also demonstrates the interest the emperor had in keeping the palaces closely connected.

During various times in his life, he lived in different rooms of the Alhambra. Hence, we can observe some stairs in the left wing of the palace that lead to various gates and fences.

The hallway leading to the room of secrets has some spaces and gaps in the thick wall, with windows that allow a view of the distant reservoir.

The Mexuar room brings together two architectures and two conceptions of the world that are very different yet very similar within the Alhambra complex.

HIDDEN SYMBOLISM OF THE FOUNTAIN OF THE LIONS

8

Palace of the Alhambra

> ## 12 lions, like the 12 tribes of Israel...

On the patio of the Palace of the Lions, built within the Alhambra in 1377 by Mohammed V, son of Yusuf I, you'll find the Fountain of the Lions, which, in cosmological symbolism, represents the Thrones (or Lions of Fire), the highest of the twelve theological levels of spiritual hierarchy.

The fountain depicts twelve lions (dating from the 11th century) which, in anthropogenetic symbolism (the study of the origin of the human species) represent the 12 tribes of Israel before they split into Jews and Arabs, the descendants of two different children: Isaac for the Jews and Ishmael for the Arabs. Arabs and Jews all descend from Abraham, who serves as the point of union between Jewish and Islamic theology as well as the mystical traditions of these two religions, Sufism and Kaballah, which infuse the twelve tribes of Israel with esoteric significance. The figures also represent the twelve signs of the zodiac, whose central sun is symbolised by the lion, demonstrating the illumination and irradiation of human and spiritual life. In Jewish belief, they also represent the sovereign kingdom of God's Chosen People, as given to Abraham the patriarch. Two of the lions have a triangle on their forehead indicating the two elite tribes: Judah and Levi.

Some authors indicate that this fountain might have been a kind of water clock marking the hours of the ablutions. The poet Ibn Gabirol (12th century) provides an almost exact description of the fountain. According to the latest studies, the lions came from the home of the Jewish grand vizier, Yusuf Ibn Nagrela (1066), who had been accused of wishing to build a palace larger than that of the caliph.

THE LEGEND OF THE TALISMAN OF THE PATIO OF THE LIONS

The marvellous legends of the Alhambra, our eternal legacy from the Moors who lived in this enchanted site, leave listeners wide-eyed. The legend of the Patio of the Lions tells the story of an Arab princess called Zaira, who lived in the Alhambra. She was beautiful, intelligent and sensitive, the complete opposite of her father who was cold, cruel, nasty and tight-fisted.

The princess adored Granada and enjoyed living in the Alhambra, although her father hated the city and the palace. He felt more African and she felt more Andalusian. She was forbidden from leaving the palace and she was alone, spending most of her time in the patio, wearing a talisman around her neck. One day, she was surprised by a handsome young man who jumped over the palace wall and told her he had seen her from afar and fallen in love with her. Surprised, she begged the young man, Arthur, to leave because her father or one of his eleven most trusted men could arrive at any moment and they would be sure to cut off his head. Arthur left, but promised that he would return.

Arthur did return, but the king saw him and imprisoned him in the dungeons. The princess went to her father's rooms to beg for mercy. She didn't find him there but she saw her father's diary on the table. In it she read that her talisman was actually under an evil spell cast by her mother shortly before she had been sent to her death by her husband. This spell fell over the king and his eleven most trusted men.

Zaira called the king and his eleven warriors to the patio where she spent her days and, sobbing, asked her father if it was true.

The king replied that indeed it was true – in the presence of his eleven men he was certain that Zaira wouldn't dare to touch the talisman.

Zaira then reminded him that her unfortunate mother had foretold that on the day her daughter learned the truth something terrible would happen to the girl's father and his faithful servants. She felt the talisman spring to life and gain strength. Then, with the roar of a lion, the king and his eleven men were turned into the twelve stone lions that surround the fountain.

From that day, the patio has been called the Patio of the Lions. Zaira freed Arthur and they lived happily ever after.

CABALISTIC SYMBOLISM OF THE ALHAMBRA

The Arab Zirí and Nasrid families (whose ancestors were direct descendants of the Ansa kings of Medina, companions of the Prophet Mohammad) moved into the Alhambra, creating a centre of culture and science that dominated the south of the Iberian Peninsula. A very large part of the hermetic, alchemic and cabalistic knowledge of the Islamic intellectuals that circulated here is expressed in the decoration of the Alhambra, revealing an artistic profusion based on sacred Islamic architecture. The most ancient part of the Alhambra palace complex is the *alcazaba,* which constituted the centre of defence and vigilance for the fortifications. It was home to the *marabous* (warrior monks), some of whom, having reached a profound knowledge of the faith, achieved saintly status. This Islamic religious knighthood dedicated itself to the esoteric arts and met in secret locations within the *alcazaba*, which was a warren of labyrinthine passages. Its subterranean area is so enormous that one could easily become lost there. This actually happened to one German visitor in November 1878, who was lost for eight days until the guards heard his cries and were able to save him from certain death. According to a popular legend, these subterranean caverns were built at night by torchlight.

The heritage of hermetic knowledge (and resulting spiritual powers) was regularly transmitted from master to disciple and then the disciples would become masters with their own disciples. This transmission of knowledge among the initiated is called *Baraka,* a Sufi concept that emphasizes the importance within Islam of spiritual knowledge leading to union with God.

The Palace of the Comares Tower, which forms part of the Alhambra, is home to the Barca Room, whose name derives from *Baraca.* The ancient Throne Room of the Alhambra is replete with very discrete kabbala symbolism, as is the arched portico of the Salon of the Ambassadors, where the caliph Nasrid would receive delegations from other kingdoms. Visitors were astonished by the beauty of these salons, in which every wall was decorated in a blaze of colours and with elaborate plasterwork featuring the Nasrid crest and Arabic inscriptions of the word "blessings" and the motto of the Nasrid kingdom: *Only God is Victorious.*

The wooden roof was decorated with a central star (Venus) representing the eye of Allah, around which the constellations swirl; the cupola reproduces the celestial heavens with the cosmic symbolism of the Seven Heavens mentioned in the Koran (*Suras* 2.29 and 23.86). More than just decoration in the hermetic style that was in vogue in Renaissance Europe at the time (see the other guides published in this series: *Secret Florence, Secret Rome, Secret Venice),* the objective was to attract to Earth, beneath the painted roof, the celestial energy it represented.

Just over the royal throne and aligned with it, we find the *Sura of the Dawn,* to protect the king from envy. Below the celestial cupola covering the salon, we find the *Sura of the Dominion,* which describes Allah as the Creator and invites the faithful to contemplate Creation through meditation. This cosmic symbolism is repeated in the Patio of the Reservoir and in the Patio of the Myrtles, whose seven gates correspond to the Seven Gates of Islam: *Firdaus* (the highest), *'Adn, Na 'iim, Na 'wa, Darussalamam, Daarul* and *Al-Muqqamul.* There is also an "eighth heaven" (*Khuldi*), the lowest region, which reflects the others, represented by an enormous reservoir that fills all the empty space of the patio.

The Islamic concept of the Seven Heavens is inspired directly by Jewish kabbala theology which calls it *Araboth* (the highest), *Machón* (I Kings 7:30, Deuteronomy 28:12), *Ma'on* (Deuteronoomy 26:15, Psalms 42:9), *Zebul* (Isaiah 63:15, I Kings 8:13), *Shehaqim* (Psalms 78:23), *Raki'a* (Genesis 1:17) and *Vilon* (Isaiah 40:22). There is also an "eighth region" called *Sheol* (Genesis 37:35). In this way, after receiving celestial energy in the Throne Room, the visitor would see the passage open symbolically to the seven heavens and paradise.

The cosmic meaning of the divine Universe, ordered by the Supreme Being, Allah or God, appears again in the beautiful Mozarabic vaults of the Room of the Two Sisters and the Abencerrajes Room, always with the Arabic motto: "Only God is victorious!" These words contain the meaning of Psalm 115 of the Bible: "Not unto us, O Lord, not unto us, but to your name be the glory!"

THE ROYAL RAWDA

Partal Gardens

> **The mystery of the empty tombs**

The royal cemetery of the Alhambra, known as the Royal *Rawda* (cemetery in Arabic), still exists. The construction of the Palace of Charles V in 1574 destroyed the cemetery. Only four pillars of a small temple and a few empty tombs survived. The niches were covered and protected by basalt gravestones with Moorish calligraphy, which are now in the Alhambra museum.

Nothing is known about the bodies once encased in the 65 graves located there, as the Royal *Rawda* of the Alhambra was found empty in 1926, as if it were a pharaoh's looted tomb. The conservator of the Alhambra, Leopoldo Towers Balbás, discovered three bodies wrapped in shrouds with some inscriptions in Arabic that indicated the noble lineage of those buried there. He tried to find the remains of the Nasrid dynasty, which, as far as we know, were moved by Boabdil to the nearby village of Mondújar, specifically to the mosque, which today is a Christian church (see below).

All we can see today are some trapezoidal tombs, built from brick and covered with plaster, with the tighter point at the feet. The cadavers rest on their right side, facing south-east in the direction of Mecca. Only a few ruins remain, but there are many legends of the bodies of kings travelling even after their deaths.

THE LAST NASRID EXILE

Some documents still exist showing that Boabdil, the last Nasrid king, was authorised by King Ferdinand and Queen Isabella to move the remains of his ancestors to the village of Mondújar, some 30 kilometres outside of Granada. Boabdil returned there one year later to bury his wife Morayma. Other sources claim that Boabdil exhumed the bodies again and took them with him during his second and final exile to Fez (Morocco) or Tlemecén (Argelia), where they were supposedly buried.

The definitive royal tombs were never found, although in the 1990s some mortal remains were discovered when land was moved to build a motorway. The mystery remains.

THE FIRST TOMB OF ISABELLA THE CATHOLIC ⑩

Parador San Francisco Royal de la Alhambra
Partal Gardens
Interior patio
• Tel: 958 221 440
• Open every day 10am-10pm

> **A queen
> who was buried
> twice**

Until 1521, the ancient convent built by the Franciscans inside the Alhambra, currently occupied by the Parador San Francisco, housed the first tomb of Queen Isabella the Catholic. She was given a provisional burial while awaiting completion of the crypt in the Royal chapel, where the mortal remains of her husband would be laid to rest. Thus, her express desire was fulfilled, to remain forever in Granada, the city that she loved "more than my own life", as she wrote.

Following the move, a plaque was left to commemorate the queen whose devout faith was expressed until her final hours (see below). On the floor of the building's beautiful Andalusian patio, which serves as a reminder that this was a Nasrid palace before becoming a monastery, we can read the inscription "Queen Isabella the Catholic was buried here".

The Convent of San Francisco, built by the queen herself in 1492, maintained a good part of its primitive original construction, unaltered when it was left to the Franciscans. Two of Granada's most illustrious citizens, Count Infantas and Antonio Gallego y Burín, ensured that it was kept in good order until it was eventually transformed to become a *Parador Nacional* (government-sponsored inn). One can still see many original Mozarabite features, such as the cistern and the magnificent gardens, which offer an unusual and unique view of the Alhambra below.

THE CATHOLIC DEATH OF QUEEN ISABELLA

After reigning for thirty years, Isabella of Castile died on 26 November 1504 at the age of 53 in her palace in Medina del Campo. Dressed in a Franciscan habit and laid out in a humble leather coffin, the Catholic queen honoured her faith in the cortege that set out along the route towards Granada following her funeral, in accordance with her royal order issued on 12 October 1504. The journey lasted 21 days.

Bells rang out across the city to receive the royal coffin as it entered by the Elvira Gate, where the Count of Tendilla, Archbishop Fray Hernando de Talavera and other city dignitaries awaited her arrival surrounded by attendants dressed in black and carrying candles.

The cortege travelled through the city up to the Alhambra. In the presbytery of the convent, the queen was buried "below the floor" in a grave marked by a plaque with a simple inscription honouring her until her body was moved to the Royal chapel.

THE SILOS OF THE GENERALIFE ⓫

Generalife
Access by the Alhambra ticket office
Included in general admission to the Alhambra

The Christian dungeons

The dungeons of the Alhambra maintain the memory of the suffering of many Christians who spent years of imprisonment there, housed in ancient silos used by the Arabs for this lugubrious purpose.

Initially, these cylindrical structures in the basement were used to store grain, spices and other household supplies. Later used as prisons, many of them are located outside the fortifications, but there are others up to seven metres high in the esplanade of the Generalife. The macabre use that was made of them in the Muslim period remains largely unknown.

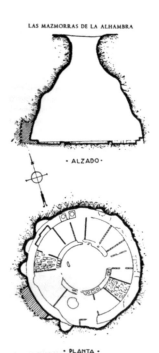

LAS MAZMORRAS DE LA ALHAMBRA

· ALZADO ·

· PLANTA ·

From inside, we can appreciate their shape (like a bottle neck or bell), some eight metres in diameter, divided into small square spaces that acted as bunks where the prisoners would sleep with their heads resting on a stone pillow.

The centre of the vault, illuminated by a single opening, had a hole to evacuate human waste.

During the day, the prisoners were taken out with ropes to work as slaves in the construction of the fortifications. At night they would return to their prison, which they could only leave if their family paid a ransom, which was calculated based on the prisoner's social status. This income was very important to the Nasrid kingdom.

The silos held up to 200 prisoners. When the Alhambra fell to the Christian troops of the Reconquista, it held a total of 7,000 prisoners.

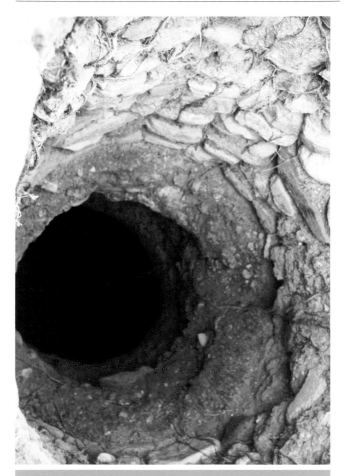

THE LEGEND OF THE HIDDEN TREASURE

Writers such as Washington Irving and Serafín Estébanez Calderón recount the tale that, when leaving the Alhambra and attempting to gather up his riches from their hiding place in the tower of the Seven Floors, Boabdil made one soldier the eternal guardian of the treasure.

A magician then cast a spell to make the treasure invisible to Christians, thereby also making the unfortunate soldier a prisoner. But the king was merciful and allowed the soldier to leave once every three years.

During this time, as long as he was accompanied by a Christian princess and a fasting priest carrying a basket of sweets (without trying to consume any of them along the route), the soldier could search for someone to pay his ransom.

MUSLIM FUNERAL PLAQUES IN THE WALL OF THE ALHAMBRA

(12)

Gate of Justice
Plaza de los Aljibes
• Entry free

> *A macabre form of humiliation for the vanquished*

Along the corridor between the Gate of Justice and plaza de los Aljibes, if you look carefully, towards the right you can see some bricks at medium height with a slightly different filigree design. The long sections carved in Malahá stone and decorated with Arab inscriptions are more delicate. They also stand out due to their lighter colour compared to the usual dusty pink used in the Alhambra.

The bricks are *maqabriyas*, Arab funeral plaques that were re-used in the construction of walls or passages by the Christian masters of the Alhambra after the Reconquista. Together with the stonemasons, the *alarifes* (architects)

contracted for the construction works made use of Arab prisoners for their labour. To make the labour even more difficult, they were forced to suffer the terrible humiliation of having to remove the funeral plaques of their own loved ones from the *rawda* (Muslim cemetery) to be re-used in the wall they were being forced to build. This form of sacrilege was common practice in the reconstruction of Arab buildings in Granada following the Reconquista. Locals were often employed as stonemasons as they were expert builders.

There are other similar examples within the Alhambra's fortifications, such as the flooring of the Patio of the Myrtles, although the restoration work carried out by Rafael Contreras replaced it with the marble paving stones visible today.

In the city, in the church of Saint Christopher in the Albaicín and in the Monastery of San Jerónimo, plaques from Elvira Gate cemetery, the largest in the city, have been re-used.

STATUE OF WASHINGTON IRVING ⓵⓷

Alhambra Woods

> *The American who dreamt the Alhambra*

Fifty years after his death, the romantic traveller of the Alhambra, Washington Irving, continues to breathe the perfume of that dream, at least symbolically in the form of the sculpture that the managers of the complex have erected in homage to the writer who celebrated the excellence of the Alhambra.

Only those who access the palace on foot will see this bronze statue by the artist Julio López, as it is found on the steep hill running from Plaza Nueva and the Granada Gate. The working tools of the first professional writer of history are included in this work, which surprises passers-by midway along the route surrounded by hundred-year-old oak trees. The legacy of the "son of the Alhambra", as he is described on the base of the statue, consists of the many tales he narrated of bandits, gypsies, songs, dances, the orientalism of the Mosque of Cordova, the unrivalled beauty of the Alhambra of Granada, the Giralda tower and the Alcázar of Seville, as well as Moguer, Palos and the Rábida.

WASHINGTON IRVING

Today, Washington Irving is synonymous worldwide with the romantic Alhambra. He spent a relatively brief but mythical stay in Granada, invited by the Russian consul. Irving spent a great deal of his life in Europe, exploring the roots of Spain's Arab soul.

In February 1826, he arrived in Spain inspired by the cultivated American ambassador to the Spanish court and admirer of Christopher Columbus, Alexander Everett. His aim was to research the great transatlantic deeds of the Italian adventurer.

On 1 March 1828, Irving began an eighteen-month adventure in Andalusia, where he remained until 23 August 1929, planning to work at the General Archive of the Indies in Seville. "A sharp tongue is the only tool used at court which is sharpened by constant use," commented Irving, as he sought to present the enchantment of southern Spain to the entire world.

A prolific writer and indefatigable traveller, his pen has written many great legends, such as the *Tales of the Alhambra:* a series of stories that attracted curious pilgrims from all over the world to Granada. In the year 1857, he re-wrote his work, adding a description of his journey to the Alhambra and his stay in the rooms of the Emperor, where he did his writing.

When he visited Granada, the palace was dilapidated and populated by humble folk. These locals were the guardians of the Alhambra and they shared with Irving all the legends of the fortress, which he immortalized on the page in the historical and legendary tone that he attributed to the people of Spain, heirs to the peninsula's Muslim past.

NIGHT WALKS THROUGH THE SABIKA WOODS ⑭

Tel: 670 309 056
- www.lawebdeidea.org
- Limited places, reservation required.
- Duration: 2.5 hours
- Admission: 10€ (8 € for the retired, students, unemployed and members of the Andalusia's Museum of Memory or Youth Card holders)

Night eyes

This interesting night walk through the Alhambra Woods, guided by specialists with in-depth knowledge of the local natural environment, allows visitors to gain a new perspective on the city's largest park. There are few opportunities to enjoy this type of alternative exploration in Granada but IDEA, the local promoter of this initiative, attracts curious visitors to the darkness and silence of the Alhambra by night. Most of the

participants already know the city very well but wish to know if better.

Walking around one-hundred-year-old elms, which, despite a rare illness, still survive; stepping over the leafy weeds that inhabit these woods, half urban and half untamed; walking along ground that is permanently fertilised by a thick layer of leaves that fall from the trees; breathing in the humidity of the daily watered park; listening to the songs of the indigenous birds (blackbirds, owls, buzzards): these are just some of the enchanting aspects of this very special excursion.

The night transforms the shapes of places that are easily recognisable by day; when the sun sets, they become a separate world in which your fantasy can complete what is only imagined in the darkness.

A TRIP TO SABIKA MOUNTAIN

The Alhambra sits upon a network of mountains. Also known as Sabika, this is an immense block of varied stones (granite, quartzite, chalk), mixed with sandstone and clay. Its extension is considerable and exploring it by night can make an appealing adventure for those who wish to walk through the most hidden areas.

THE KEY AND THE HAND AT THE GATE OF JUSTICE

15

Gate of Justice
• Entry free

> *When the hand takes the key, Granada will be Muslim again*

A key and a hand are carved at equal heights into the arch of the entrance to the Gate of Justice. The key is associated with the legend of the Arab magician and astrologist who, after hitting it with the knob of his staff, disappeared into the bowels of the earth with a slave, a singer and harpist with whom he was in love. The slave symbolized the Alhambra whose beauty is capable of captivating anyone. The magician represents the hermetic sciences, to which the key allows access.

The key is an important symbol for the Alhambra because it represents the faith that energised the powers conferred upon the Prophet Mohammad for the spread of Islam. The hand is probably the famous "Hand of Fatima" (the fifth daughter of the Prophet), whose five fingers represent the five fundamental pillars of Islam (Faith, Prayer, Charity, Fasting, Pilgrimage) and the five daily prayers of the faithful.

THE LEGEND OF THE GATE OF JUSTICE

According to legend, the Gate of Justice was so solid and perfect that the Alhambra could be besieged by thousands of enemy armies without ever being breached. However, if the key of the inner arch of the Gate of Justice ever met with the hand in the outer arch, the end of the world would be nigh. Legend claims that the magnificence of the Arch of Justice was such that no soldier on horseback could harm the hand sculpted on the top of the arch with his lance. Those who made this claim were so certain of it that they declared anyone doing so would conquer the throne of the Alhambra.

SYMBOLISM OF THE PILLAR OF CHARLES V 🔟

Next to the Gate of Justice
Alhambra Woods

*Charles V
and hermetism*

ocated near the Gate of Justice, the Pillar of Charles V (known as Pillar of the Cornetas in the 17th century) is built against a wall dating from 1568 that was part of the defences of the Alhambra. By order of Charles V, and financed by the Count of Tendilla, the pillar was designed by the architect Pedro Machuca of Granada in 1543 and built by the Milanese artist Niccolo da Corte.

In 1624, local sculptor Alonso de Mena restored it on the occasion of a visit to Granada by Philip IV. It contains various references to alchemy, a science that the Portuguese King Manuel I practised with great interest, giving rise to the term "manueline hermeticism." Manuel I was the father of Isabella of Portugal, the wife of Charles V, and probably exercised a strong influence over his son-in-law, sharing his esoteric knowledge with the court of Granada.

The first part of the pillar is divided into three sections, separated by

pilasters decorated with branches of pomegranate and the Tendilla coat of arms on the laterals. The Old Testament makes reference thirteen times to the pomegranate, always referring to it as a life-giving symbol, due to its juice and many seeds. King Salomon considered it the fruit of love, idealised in the Queen of Saba.

In the centre of the ensemble, there are three large masked heads crowned with wheat sheafs, flowers and fruit, representing the three seasons that symbolise the three rivers of Granada: summer for the Darro, spring for the Beiro and autumn for the Genil. However, alchemists related these seasons to the three stages of great work: black work (initial stage) for autumn; white work (intermediate stage) for spring; red work (final stage) for summer.

The second section contains in its centre the words *Imperatori Caesari Karolo quinto Hispaniarum regí* (Emperor Caesar, Charles V, King of Spain).

Indeed, Charles V also was called Caesar (or Caesar Charles), referring to the ancient Caesars, as he was the Holy Roman Emperor. The words are flanked by the coats of arms of Burgundy and Lorraine with the Columns of Hercules and two crossed branches, symbolising the Order of the Golden Fleece to which the monarch belonged.

In alchemical symbolism, crossed branches represent the vapour of mercury, or the point at which gold begins to emerge as liquid in the distillation stage, before taking its definitive form. This also represents the final and definitive conquest of the hermetic world, when the alchemist becomes Emperor of Nature (*Natura Imperator*), having reached a state of enlightenment.

The Columns of Hercules are also a metaphor considered by some alchemists to represent the final step towards achieving the great work of alchemy that creates the philosopher's stone, synonymous with spiritual achievement in the perfection of nature.

On both sides, an angel holds a dolphin that spouts water and below, two more angels pour water on snails. In alchemy, the dolphin is a traditional symbol of the philosopher's stone, which rises from the waters of Life like the vapour of mercury. The snail alludes to the primordial sound (the "Word") that marked the beginning of Creation. The Gospel of Saint John begins: "In the principio was the Word, in the Word was with God..."

Topping off the symbolism, the imperial coat of arms of Charles V with the two-headed Hapsburg, adorned with the motto *Plus ultra* (still further), is a reference to his vast empire, which extended across almost all of Europe. In this context, the motto can even be taken to mean going beyond human comprehension, an idea reinforced by the cherub at the top of the image, as "cherubim", from the Hebrew kerub, means "hidden treasure".

The wall above which the pillar rests contains four relief medallions depicting Hercules killing the Lernaean Hydra (an allusion to the emperor's

Christian fidelity, victorious over the infidels); the sisters Frixo and Hele crossing the Hellespont (Straight of the Dardanelles) astride a ram (a reference to the legend of the establishment of the Order of the Golden Fleece); Daphne followed by Apollo (indicating the solar empire of Charles V) with Apollo representing the sun and Daphne being daughter of Gaia (the Earth); and Alexander the Great (emperor of almost all the ancient world, comparable to Charles V, emperor of the European Renaissance).

For more information about the Order of the Golden Fleece in alchemy, see page 155.

THE ORDER OF THE GOLDEN FLEECE

According to René Alleau, a historian of esoteric tradition, the destiny of the Order of the Golden Fleece was "to re-establish the initial links between East and West destroyed by the Order of the Temple". Various Belgian and French nobles responsible for the establishment of the Order had very close relations with the ancient Templars, abolished in 1312. The constitution of the Order also stated that it should "honour the ancient knights whose noble deeds are worthy of recognition", which seems to be a veiled reference to the ancient Knights Templar.

On 10 January 1429, on the occasion of his wedding to Princess Isabella of Portugal, daughter of King John I, Philip III (the Good), Duke of Burgundy, established the Chivalric Order of the Golden Fleece "in homage to the Virgin Mary and the Apostle Saint Andrew". The solemn ceremony took place in the Basilica of the Holy Blood in Bruges, Belgium. According to the historian Baron Reinffenberg, "a live sheep painted blue with its horns covered in gold thread" walked among the guests, symbolising the "Lamb of God that takes away the sin of the world", Jesus Christ.

The Order met 22 times before gradually converting into what it is today "an honorific order without any specific spiritual or initiation rites". This development began with the death of King Charles II of Spain (1661-1700) and the War of Spanish Succession. The Order was divided in two: the Spanish faction and the Austrian faction. Each claimed historical legitimacy. The former king Albert II of Belgium is a rare example of a knight of both factions.

Originally, the Order of the Golden Fleece followed hermetic tradition, and especially alchemy, based on the Greek myth of Jason the Argonaut, who received the golden fleece from the winged ram. The golden fleece was found hanging from a sacred oak in the mountains of the southern Caucasus, according to Homer's account dating from the 13th century B.C. The fleece, shorn by Jason, represents the search for spiritual treasure and divine wisdom. Jason symbolised the alchemist capable of creating the philosopher's stone, which is to say, achieving the quintessential alchemy laboratory. He is the prototype of the enlightened wise man.

The myth of the establishment of the Order of the Golden Fleece is associated with the Apostle Saint Andrew, who evangelised the country when Jason went looking for the ram. Saint Andrew is also the patron saint of alchemists, associated with Mary who symbolises raw material and Christ who symbolises the philosopher's stone.

From the 11th century, the Greek Suda, in his *Lexicon*, proposed an interpretation of the alchemy of Jason. In 1730, in Germany, Ehrd of Naxagoras wrote a treatise on alchemy entitled *Orden Goldenes Vliess* ("Order of the Golden Fleece"). Some years later, in 1749, Hermann Fictuld published a new study on alchemy with the same title.

He sets out the alchemic symbolism of Jason's travels in a precise and systematic manner, with an analysis of the content and hermetic meaning of the Order of the Golden Fleece. According to Cornelio Agrippa (1486-1535), Philip the Good created the Order of the Golden Fleece specifically to honour the mysteries of alchemy. Fictuld analysed the symbolism of all the rituals prescribed for use in the ceremonies of the Order, which reinforced Agrippa's comments.

On the first day of the festival of the Order, the celebration of the General Chapter, the knights would make a visit to the sovereign wearing purple, the colour of spiritual level, and gold, representing yellow work (*citredo* in Latin) and the affirmation of their spiritual dignity.

On the second day, the feast of Saint Andrew, they would wear black, symbolising black work *[nigredo]* or the original colour of the raw material. The third day, in commemoration of the splendour of the Mother of God, they wore white, representing white work *(albedo)* or purification of the soul. Red *[rubedo]* was the colour of their daily habit, while purple is the colour worn by penitents as they purify themselves through fasting and prayer before participating in any great celebration of communion with the Divine. After preparation, they are transformed during the celebration: they begin wearing black, then change into white and finally red.

The order of these colours follows the chronological sequence of the colours of the process of alchemy: black, white, red. When preparing the great work, the raw material begins to putrefy and becomes black. When it is heated, it then turns white, the colour of light and silver. With the continuous action of the secret fire of the philosophers (symbolised by the Sheep), the white of perfection becomes red, which then turns a translucent purple, indicating the final step in producing the philosopher's stone.

The distinctive emblem of the Order of the Golden Fleece is a collar of gold with eight golden elements, each decorated with two rifles from which the insignia of the Order hangs: a medal displaying a ram dressed in the golden fleece.

On penalty of mutilation, all knights of the Order were obliged to wear a collar, which no one else could use. During battles, they could wear the collar without the fleece. When it was damaged, it had to be repaired immediately by goldsmiths and while it was being repaired, the knight would be excused from wearing it and paying the penalty. It was forbidden to adorn the collar with any other jewel or ornament. It could not be sold or given as a gift or pawned under any circumstances. If a knight were to lose it, another one must be made at his own expense; if it was stolen from him on the battlefield, the king would give him a new one. In the case of death or expulsion from the Order, the collar would be handed over within three months to the treasurer of the Order.

Hermann Fictuld also understood the collar of golden fleece as symbolic of the vellum roll on which the ancients would write in letters of gold about science, and alchemy in particular. As well as the collar, the knights of the Order of the Golden Fleece also wore a six-pointed star on their chest, formed by two superimposed triangles: a symbol of elemental alchemy with double meaning.

Thus, the four natural elements (Earth, Water, Fire, Air) are represented as the union of the Water "Queen" (triangle with apex facing downwards) and the Fire "King" (triangle with the apex facing upwards). For alchemists, the hexagram thus formed is the famous star of *Azot,* the mercury of the philosophers, and *Ignis,* the philosophical fire that transforms everything.

PASSAGES BELOW THE RODRÍGUEZ-ACOSTA **⑰** FOUNDATION

Callejón del Niño del Royo
• Tel: 958 227 497
• www.fundacionrodriguezacosta.com
• info@fundacionrodriguezacosta.com
• Open: 8:30am-5pm (Mar 15 - Oct 14) and 10am-3:30pm (Oct 15 - Mar 14)
• Entry: 5€

Underground escape

The basement of the Villa Rodríguez-Acosta contains approximately 800 metres of passages with steep stairs built by the constructor and owner, painter José Maria Rodríguez-Acosta. Its good state of conservation is due to the artistic sensitivity of its owner, who decorated the corridors with free-standing columns and round arches, adding mouldings and vases, as well as beautifying this substantial villa and the site with a reservoir, an enormous neoclassical frieze and a substantial colonnade.

With scarce documentation about these passages, no one knows their exact purpose. According to the managers of the establishment, there is very little information in the drawings and plans for construction, dating from the first decade of the 20th century. However, they could be the extension of city dungeons or perhaps a route used by prisoners to escape.

Open to visitors along the route are various passages, all of them encased so that the earth is visible as well as the varying substrata of the mountain within which the route progresses via a steep staircase downhill. Amphorae can be seen in the nooks and crannies of the grottos as far as the modernised final landing.

Throughout these subterranean passages, one can appreciate how the city lived. In these depths, in the dark ages and the medieval period, it was as if Granada awaited visits from the curious in order to offer them its mystery and most-hidden secrets.

BERMEJA TOWERS

Visible from the exterior

The Bermeja Towers are located at the top of Mauror Hill, with views over all Granada and the countryside, including the neighbourhoods of Realejo and Albaicín, populated by the unruly Moors. One can see the "red towers" which provided defence and were originally part of the now vanished Hizn Mawror castle. One wall, which no longer exists in its original form, linked it to the *alcazaba* to make it easier to send reinforcements through a horseshoe arch that can still be seen today. The cistern below the complex is also visible from the exterior. Throughout the 20th century, the towers were used as a military prison, holding prisoners during the Spanish Civil War and more in later decades.

ARCH OF THE EARS

18

Alhambra Woods
Gomérez Hill

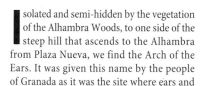

*An arch
where ears
would hang*

I solated and semi-hidden by the vegetation of the Alhambra Woods, to one side of the steep hill that ascends to the Alhambra from Plaza Nueva, we find the Arch of the Ears. It was given this name by the people of Granada as it was the site where ears and other body parts amputated from delinquents would be displayed, although its actual name was Bib- Rambla (River Gate) arch.

In actual fact, the gate doesn't lead anywhere. It is lost in a no-man's land but maintained for the future, far from the mundane noise of Bib-Rambla square. It was one of the entry gates to the walled city, in one of the busiest sites of Arab Granada, close to the souk, the mosque and the vitality of a bustling city full of life.

AN ARCH TORN DOWN THEN REBUILT

The Arch of the Ears was almost destroyed. Granada adored progress and had little interest in ancient stones, but the odyssey involved in saving this monument ended with the arch's move to its current site.

In 1873, the Town Hall ordered its destruction, hoping to avoid the strong opposition of artists and intellectuals such as the local journalist Luis Seco de Lucena, but they were not successful. In 1881, it was declared a national monument, yet in 1884 the government of Cánovas del Castillo, at that time director of the Royal Academy of History, ordered its total destruction, apparently due to hygiene concerns. As is often the case in Granada when it's a question of disturbing a historic site, a grassroots movement took action against the plan to dismantle the arch and move it to the Archaeological Museum, where it would be forgotten. Finally, the director of the Alhambra and Generalife, Leopoldo Towers Balbás, placed it at its current site in the 1930s, but sadly the interior vaults have been lost.

THE CHILD OF THE PILLAR

Callejón Niño del Royo

A macabre joke

Until the first half of the 19th century, when looking out from Mauror Hill one could see an elongated figure that appeared to be a head over a body with its arms at its sides. Whenever anyone asked about what appeared to be a child standing next to the road, the locals jokingly replied that it was "the child of the pillar". However, when travellers approached the figure, they could see that the arms were actually hooks from which hung human remains. And what they believed to be a child was a column or pillar that held the remains of convicted criminals, to serve as an example for others.

The lord of the Alhambra had his own pillars in Niño del Royo (Child of the Pillar) alley as a warning to dissuade citizens from any delinquent temptations. The name of the street is the only remnant of a time when justice was applied without much reflection. That justice included amputations of hands, feet, arms and even heads, as well as other savage sentences of that period: mutilation, hanging, quartering, etc.

Until the end of the Pre-Napoleonic times, one could find these "pillars of justice" in Spain: posts with hooks on the sides and a royal or aristocratic coat of arms. These monuments to torture were also the physical indication that the village held power to administer justice or that, from this point on, the law was enforced by another authority (royal, ecclesiastical, military or civil).

A FRATERNITY TO COLLECT HUMAN REMAINS

These sites offered a macabre spectacle along Spanish roads and in the cities. In the city of Granada, there were around ten of them at various points, usually surrounded by rodents or buzzards enjoying a good feast. According to historical records, until the 18th century some compassionate citizens organised themselves into the Fraternity of Peace and Charity. The fraternity would travel through the city streets with barrows and carts collecting human remains to take to a sacred site where, after offering a mass and reciting an "Our Father" for these unfortunate souls, they would give them Christian burial.

FORMER DOOR OF A PHOTOGRAPHY SHOP

Exterior wall of the Villa of the Martyrs

The abandoned entrance to an old photography shop is one of the last remaining illustrations of the Alhambra's popularity at the turn of the 20th century, when tourism began to emerge in this corner of Andalusia.

Photographers in the Alhambra

Few vestiges remain of the avalanche of tourism that arrived in Granada between the end of the 19th century and the beginning of the 20th century. All that remains is the entrance to what was once a lucrative business owned by Meersman, a Belgian engineer with a passion for the new art form of the 20th century. Meersman opened a photographic laboratory in his villa with a shop for tourists. The shop was located in a portion of the wall around the Villa of the Martyrs, in a street that rises from the avenue to this lovely garden. The imitation Arab arch, typical of the period, can still be seen. We can also observe the desire to reproduce the splendour of Andalusia in the use of *azulejos* and brick still visible in the wall.

When tourism arrived in southern Spain, it was popular for visitors to have their portrait taken in Moorish dress, especially along the hill leading to the entrance of the fortifications, where thousands of visitors passed in search of exoticism and oriental adventure.

Books like Washington Irving's *Tales of the Alhambra* and the hundreds of drawings, photographs and tales from romantic travellers who visited Granada piqued the public's interest in Europe's only Arab palace. Its intense popularity was inevitable.

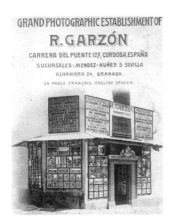

GROTTO OF THE VIRGIN OF LOURDES

Camino Nuevo del Cementerio, s/n
Grotto of the Virgin
Barranco del Abogado

> *The virgin
> of the cave*

For more than a century, the interior of a natural cave in the Barranco del Abogado neighbourhood held a small replica of the Virgin of Lourdes (France), the most venerated image (see below). A pilgrimage is held every year on the feast day of the Virgin of Lourdes (11 February), a tradition that has gained in popularity in recent years.

Saint Cecil parish administers the chapel-cave, which contains a written plaque commemorating its construction in 1903. The small hermitage was supported financially by Pillar García Romanillos, a local woman who, like Maria Luisa de Dios, belonged to the congregation of the Redemptorists or the Apostolic Ladies, who sought to improve the life of the inhabitants of the neighbourhood, which for many years did not have the basic conditions for a decent standard of living.

A FORGOTTEN NEIGHBOURHOOD NEAR THE ALHAMBRA

Barranco del Abogado, or the Virgin of Lourdes neighbourhood, is located on the slopes of the Alhambra, in the area called Antequeruela, one of the least visited and least known neighbourhoods of the city.

The terrain is rough and there was no public telephone, post box or even bus stop until 2002. The first public fountain with drinking water was not provided for the neighbourhood until 1920 and today there is still no street lighting, nor do the houses have drinking water. Over the last thirty years the area has been improved and the small homes are being purchased and modernised inside and out.

According to census figures, there are 600 residents in Barranco del Abogado, descendants of the labourers, workers and artisans who traditionally lived here.

The inhabitants believe that the origin of the neighbourhood's name came from a lawyer who acquired the land in 1623 as payment for his services, although there is another almost forgotten legend that a knight was murdered here in the dark years of Pre-Napoleonic times.

THE TREE OF SAINT JOHN OF THE CROSS ㉒

Garden of the Villa of the Martyrs
• Open: Mon-Fri 10am-2pm and 6pm-8pm; Saturday, Sunday and
holidays 10am-8pm (Apr 1 - Oct 14); Mon-Fri 10am-2pm and 5pm-6pm;
Saturday, Sunday and holidays 10am-6pm (Oct 15 - Mar 31)

Poem in the shade of a tree

In the middle of the garden of the Villa of the Martyrs there is a 100-year-old tree whose shadow provides shelter to those seeking spiritual rest. It is said to have been planted by Saint John of the Cross, the master of Christian mysticism and the prior of the convent of the Order of the Barefoot Carmelites between 1582 and 1588. According to the legend, the saint wrote his masterpiece, *The Dark Night of the Soul,* in the shade of this tree.

Brought from Portugal, this example of the species *Cupressus Llusitanica Mili* is said to have been taken as a seedling from the sacred forest of Bussaco (province of Coimbra).

Saint John of the Cross's tree stands in the upper part of the villa's garden in a space where many centuries ago the Carmelites planted some of the rarest species of flora and fauna in the world, including this cypress, although in Granada it is referred to as a "cedar".

Apart from this enormous tree, the most ancient in the orchard, the gardens have many delightful features, including a lake with an island. There is a large tower as well as fountains, exotic and medicinal plants, an oriental garden and an Islamic patio with a lovely grotto.

Unfortunately, the convent of Saint John of the Cross was destroyed in 1842 and replaced by a small building, which today is the site of the monastery and the noviciate. All that remains of the saint is this cedar and one of the most expressive poems of Spanish literature, dedicated to God and filled with all the love a human being can feel in the dark night of the soul.

THE RAIN CISTERN
Road to the Winter Park

A cistern for the mountain rain

On the road to the Winter Park, a cistern, two thirds of which is subterranean, collects rain water, hence its name: the Rain Cistern. It was part of the extensive water collection system of the upper palaces of the Alhambra (Castle of Saint Helen, Seat of the Dark Moor, Dar al Arusa, Rota Reservoir, Western Wells, Albercón del Negro, Palace of the Alixares).

This invention stands at 930 meters above sea level (compared to 680 meters for the city of Granada) and accumulates rain channelled through a central orifice, following the *compluvium* system designed by the Romans.

It had two side entrances for water collection that were replaced over time by a more modern system. The Rain Cistern is another admirable Nasrid invention to make use of water, in this case rain from the mountains, which is a blessing for Granada.

Walking towards Llano del Perdiz, we notice a metallic access gate in the middle of the landscape. From the exterior one can observe its upper vaults above the route that served as an overflow channel for the reservoir.

The cistern, built using bricks and plaster, is square in design, measuring almost eight metres on each side.

The three pointed barrel vaults, which act as counter weights, allow for the construction of a great vaulted central space.

Drawn by the traveller Georgius Hoefnagle in 1575 for his work *Civitatis Orbis Terrarum*, the cistern was rediscovered in the 19th century in a good state of conservation and still fully functional. The Rain Cistern is still used by the city as an additional water reserve.

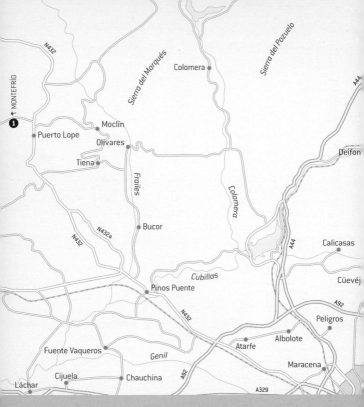

TO THE NORTH

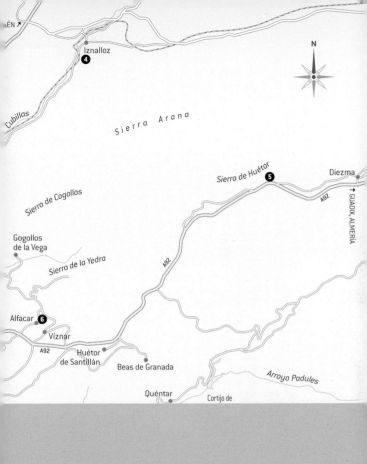

CHURCH OF THE INCARNATION IN MONTEFRIO ❶

Tel: 958 336 004 / 958 336 136
- E-mail: turismontefrio@montefrio.org
- www.montefrio.org

> **A replica of Rome's Pantheon for Japanese weddings**

The church of the Incarnation in Montefrio (from *monte ferido*, 'injured mountain') has an immense dome 30 meters in diameter over its circular base and is known locally as *la redonda* ('the round one').

This unusual neoclassical building is attributed to the architect Ventura Rodríguez, although it was actually built by his disciple Lois de Monteagudo. It is a copy of the Pantheon in Rome, the design of which was taken as a model for the construction and adapted for use as a Christian church (see comparison below). Construction was completed in just 16 years (from 1786 to 1802) during the reign of Charles III.

Next to the immense, perfectly circular nave is an additional rectangle where the principal chapel is located and a second one where the congregation enters. The disproportionate size of this temple compared to other churches indicates that it is an unusual style of architecture imported from other lands.

In 1981 Professor Yuri Oyama from the University of Yokohama visited the village of Montefrio and fell in love with the site. She lived there for a year and later visited on four other occasions. A keen photographer, in 1983 Oyama published a book of photographs and set up several exhibitions about her 'discovery'. The interest of the Japanese public in Oyama's work and the support of Japanese tour operators made Montefrio a popular tourist destination. Since then, monuments have had signs in three languages: Spanish, English and Japanese.

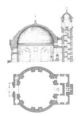

JAPANESE WEDDINGS SPANISH STYLE

The Villa of Montefrio offers Japanese couples the unique opportunity to marry in 'Spanish style'. Weddings are held in the Town Hall and the entire populace contributes so that brides and grooms arriving from Tokyo, Yokohama or Nagasaki can enjoy the authentic colours and flavours of Spanish weddings. The happy couple are showered with rice as they leave the ceremony, *jamón* is served at the banquet and *sevillana* dances add the final touch to the event.

CORTIJO DEL MARQUÉS HOTEL ❷

Camino del Marqués, s/n
18220 Albolote
• Tel: 958 340 077
• Email: reservas@cortijodelmarques.com
• www.cortijodelmarques.com
• 11 rooms, priced between 90€ -150€
Take the A-44 motorway that runs between Jaén and Granada then
exit at Deifontes (km 108). From the roundabout take the service road
running parallel to the A-44. The route is well-signposted from this
point. The hotel is located less than 4 kilometers away along a road 18
kilometers to the north of Granada.

*The
'fossilized'
farmhouse*

The Farmhouse of the Marquis of
Mondéjar is an ancient farmhouse
that has been converted into luxury
accommodation allowing guests to enjoy
the traditional lifestyle of the Andalusian
countryside. Throughout its restoration, traditional materials were used to
recreate a working farmhouse, which used to be home to both estate workers
and aristocrats from time to time.

It is almost a town in miniature. The secluded church in its centre gave
shelter to thirty field labouring families, as well as the blacksmith, miller,
school teacher and shepherds. The estate extends over 4000 hectares of
olive groves in an immense, rectilinear plain that was originally a convent

of nuns before becoming
the marquis of Mondéjar's
farmhouse. Today it
markets itself as a 'secret
farmhouse' offering luxury
accommodation for
weddings and banquets.

The magnificent
church that presides over
this village bears witness
not only to the original
convent and cloister, but
also to the importance of
religious life in rural Spain.

HOT SPRINGS IN DEIFONTES

Deifontes

3

I n the town of Deifontes, abundant waters gush in hot springs, creating a Garden of Eden in the middle of a park graced with an abundance of nature. This phenomenon gives the town its charming name: Deus-fontes (fountains of God), also Daifontes, Dayfonte, Dialfate or *dar al-font* (house or site of the fountain).

> **The fountains of God**

The geysers, surrounded by low brick walls, provide a welcome cool sensation and the serenity of a unique space. The silence is only interrupted by the flow of water surging from the depths.

The park and hot springs are at the end of the town, surrounded by the Cubillas River, which helps to shelter the garden from the noise and heat of summer. They are close to the Hermitage of San Isidro, which can be reached from the N323 motorway and from Iznalloz.

Thankfully, this site has yet to be discovered by tour operators. There is just one small hotel with wooden bungalows on the other side of the river. The only travellers reaching this far have arrived along the routes of the Andalusian League and the Nasrid – both include Deifontes as a final stop, in the middle of the Sierra de Arana, before arriving in Granada.

BIENVENIDOS·A DEIFONTES

TIERRA DE FUENTES

ELEGANT REST STOP

When carriages made stops to allow horses to drink and travellers to rest, one of the most famous and popular inns along the Royal Route of Granada was built close to the hot springs. The ancient inn was known as the *Inn of the Birth* and dated from the 13th century. Written sources tell us that even the famous mystics Christian San Juan of the Cross and Saint Teresa of Avila rested here during their long journeys to Granada.

WATER CAVE ④

Pico del Asno , Sierra Arana, Iznalloz
• Tel: 958 247 500 / 958 247 384
• E-mail: cavedelagua@dipgra.es
• Opening hours: Mon-Sat 10am-3pm
• Visit upon application to the Cultural Office of the Granada Council. Groups of 15 maximum

Ghosts in the cave

The large subterranean cavern close to the village of Iznalloz is known as the Water Cave (Sabina Cave, Donkey Cave or Deifontes Cave). Within the gigantic network of subterranean passages one finds huge formations of stalagmites and stalactites. This spectacularly deep and spooky crevice in the Sierra Arana is unique to the area known as Dragon Teeth Cavern or the Chamber of the Dragons.

Visitors can enjoy the Plus Ultra Cavern, the Juan and Charles Gallery and the University Gallery. In the Music Room there are fascinating crystallised structures shaped like coral; the Glacier Lagoon offers a magnificent petrified waterfall and there are small lagoons of pure water in the Greek Lake.

At an altitude of 1750 metres, with a drop of 180 metres and a longitude of 3000 metres, the Water Cave has a constant temperature of nine degrees. The action of the water on the limestone terrain has formed a spectacular void with steep slopes and lateral galleries. Over time, the relentless action of nature has created many huge interconnected cavities.

The caves are of both geological and biological interest as they contain as many as 23 endemic species, some of which are specific to this cave. The majority, such as the pseudo-scorpion or the myriapod *origmatogona tinautil*, are white and blind since they never see sunlight.

The universities of Andalusia conduct research in this micro-world to find the perfect balance between tourism and the preservation of the site's ecological richness.

THE MOLINILLO INN

5

Sierra de Huétor
Huétor Santillán
A-4004 (exit A-92), ancient road from Granada to Guadix

Saint
Manuel

The entire area surrounding the ancient Molinillo Inn is wrapped in a halo of magic and mystery, as the cabin of the area's most famous faith healer, 'Saint Manuel', is located just a few metres above it.

The medicine man used unusual methods, which, according to much of the evidence collected, were very effective. He did not require money in exchange for his services, so his patients would bring gifts of firewood and vehicles. Over time, the mountain of firewood beside his cabin became so huge that some feared for the safety of his home. Also, more than 300 vehicles were parked along the roads nearby (cars, motorbikes and, above all, lorries of every make and model).

The Molinillo Inn was no longer a wayside stop; it became a meeting point for those who had heard of the miraculous healing powers of this simple and very humble man.

Today, a visit to the ancient Molinillo Inn offers an opportunity to experience the Spain of the past. However, one can still see the enormous mountain of firewood, which bears witness to the rickety, humble abode of Saint Manuel.

The faith healer himself suffered from a mysterious incurable illness that left him bed ridden. At his funeral, in the town of Huétor Santillán, hundreds of mourners came from all over Spain to join his body in a silent procession from the Molinillo Inn to Huétor Santillán. A caravan of cars stretching for many kilometres honked their horns, flowers were thrown from the windows and fireworks were set off.

Saint Manuel died on 7 March 2001 and every year on the anniversary of his death hundreds of mourners visit his tomb to remember a good man who would cure anyone who went to him for help.

MONUMENT TO THE DEATH OF FEDERICO GARCÍA LORCA

6

García Lorca Park
Paraje de Fuente Grande, s/n
Alfacar

*Lorca's
lost tomb*

In 1986 the Town Hall of Alfacar began the construction of an immense park dedicated to the memory of one of Spain's most distinguished poets of the 20th century, Federico García Lorca. The park was to be built on the site where, according to popular belief, he was killed and buried.

In 2010, due to recent revisionism of the Civil War and despite the opposition of the poet's family, efforts were commenced to find his remains. However, nothing has been found in the park or in the surrounding area.

The poet's most beautiful verses have been immortalised on the walls of the central square and a monument bearing the inscription "To the memory of Federico García Lorca and all the victims of the Civil War" stands beside the olive tree which, until recently, was thought to mark the site of his burial.

On the anniversary of Lorca's death (18 August 1936), people come from all over Spain for a night of music in his honour and to leave flowers at the monument.

The only clue to the exact location of Federico's untimely death is a verse from a local song that states, "Between Víznar and Alfacar they killed a song bird because he wanted to sing". Lorca specialists and scholars, and even the local authorities of Viznar and Alfacar, are still actively searching for the poet's body.

FEDERICO, BROTHER OF THE ALHAMBRA

Few people know that the poet baptised as Federico del Sagrado Corazón de Avila García Lorca was a brother of the fraternity of the Virgin of the Alhambra. The famous local poet was one of the founding brothers of the Fraternity of the Virgin of the Angustias of the Alhambra and carried the cross at the front of the Holy Week procession in Granada in 1928, dressed as a penitent.

STUDIO OF THE ARTIST MIGUEL RUIZ JIMÉNEZ

❼

Camino Viejo def Jun, s/n
(Jun-Alfacar junction) Jun
• Tel: 958 414 077
• www.miguelruizjimenez.com
• E-mail: grupomrj@gmail.com
• Opening hours: Mon-Fri 8am-2pm and 3pm-7pm
• Visits must be reserved in advance
• Minimum 4-5 people
• Entry fee: 4€

*A dome
for art*

The pavilion built by local artist Miguel Ruiz Jiménez is a temple dedicated to ceramics and sculpture. The artist, famous for his works of golden pottery, is a true genius and self-taught artist who has enjoyed an illustrious career.

The most original aspect of this unusual structure is its grandiose dome, with a diameter of 18 metres, surrounded by a strange fence inspired by cathedral organ pipes.

Miguel Ruiz's sculptures are often gigantic and original. However, the most fascinating exhibit in his studio is the huge collection of replicas of Nasrid ceramics, each over one metre tall, that this multi-faceted artist has painstakingly reproduced.

The interior of the construction is divided into three parts, among which we find the largest sculpture of the site: an immense human figure in homage to fans of the local football team.

The garden is filled with vessels, lamps and other items inspired by the work of Nasrid ceramicists. There are classrooms and a conference centre where the sculptor gives lectures about his experience, as well as the 'artistic laboratory' where his creative work is done. He works using an innovative technique of his own invention based on chemical studies.

His Nasrid-inspired vases are displayed in some of the world's most renowned museums and he produces them here on order for as much as 50,000 euros each. His usual clients are royalty, such as the rulers of Saudi Arabia, who employed the artist in 1999 to assist with the interior decoration of a replica of the Alhambra palace in Riyad. He made a complete collection of the vases of the Alhambra and has undertaken commissions for many institutions, such as the European Parliament and Unesco. It takes four months on average to complete each commissioned piece.

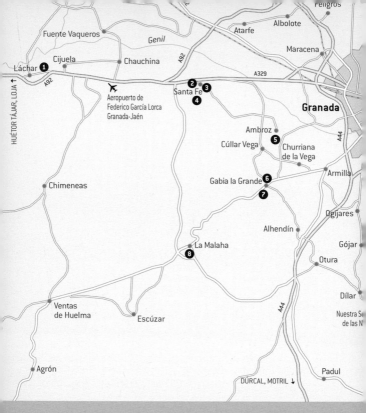

TO THE SOUTH

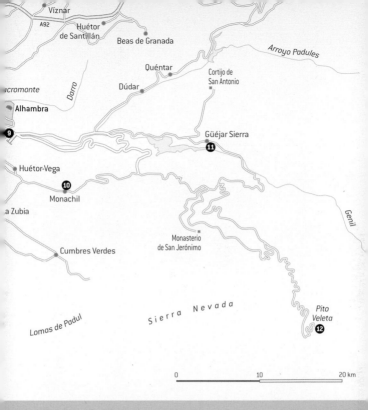

THE ROMAN TOWER IN ROMILLA ❶

Casa Real de Soto de Roma
Paseo de la Reina, s/n
Fuente Vaqueros-Valderrubio road, km 23

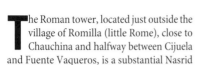

A Nasrid defensive bastion

The Roman tower, located just outside the village of Romilla (little Rome), close to Chauchina and halfway between Cijuela and Fuente Vaqueros, is a substantial Nasrid defensive bastion.

Visible from all the surrounding fields due to its great height, for centuries it marked the southernmost point of the large hunting estate known as the Royal Roman Grove (see below).

The solid appearance of the three storey quadrangle is reinforced by the absence of openings, with the exceptions of two small windows in the middle of its walls. A cistern below ground ensured the independence of the garrison that defended it in the final days of the Nasrid kingdom.

PEPE THE ROMAN

For centuries, the inhabitants of the small village of Romilla were known as "Romans". This is the origin of the name of the famous character "Pepe the Roman" in *The House of Bernarda Alba* by Federico García Lorca.

THE ROMAN GROVE

The Roman Grove was initially a Roman working estate that doubled as a hunting lodge and recreation area for the kings of Granada. It was one of the properties of the royal family, who enjoyed its dense forests and plantations. It was used by the nobility until Charles IV gave it to Manuel Godoy in exchange for a stable of horses in Aranjuez and added the title Lord of the Roman Grove and the State of Albalá to his many noble titles. During the reign of Fernando VII, all his properties were seized and the Roman Grove returned to the crown, although not for long. In the king's absence, the courts of Cádiz gave it, as well as Ciudad Rodrigo, to the Duke of Wellington as an expression of gratitude for his services in helping Spain to see off Napoleon. Until 1940 the Roman Grove and the surrounding towns (Fuente Vaqueros, Valderrubio and Romilla) belonged to the Duke, who rented the land to farm workers who were able to purchase the estate over time.

NEARBY

THE VILLA AT ROMAN GROVE

The villa at Roman Grove, currently in use for elegant celebrations of weddings and banquets, could be seen from a distance and dominated the Roman Grove estate. It is located little more than one kilometre from Fuente Vaqueros at the end of Paseo de la Reina in the direction of Valderrubio. Surrounded by an exotic garden, its rooms are sumptuous, as is the parish church of Fuente Vaqueros, a small chapel with a single nave adjacent to the villa complex. It was granted the status of parish church in 1780 and the privileges of a royal chapel until 1837.

MONUMENT TO THE INVENTOR OF THE *PIONONO* ❷

Calle Real
Santa Fe

The devout baker

The creator of the *pionono* pastry, Ceferino Isla González, not only has a town square dedicated to his memory but also a statue close to the bakery where he first produced this sweet, which has made the village of Santa Fe famous around the world.

The first *pionono* was baked in 1897 in homage to the Pope, who in 1858 propagated the dogma of the Immaculate Conception of the Virgin Mary Mother of Christ (see below) within the Catholic Church. Pope Pius IX was known as Pío Noveno for the Spanish and Pio Nono for the Italians.

The statue by sculptor Miguel Moreno from Granada, who at one time lived in the village, is a faithful reproduction of the serious figure of this devoted baker. Today, the bakery in Calle Real has become an emporium of the finest confectionary, known as Casa Isla.

The *pionono* is thought to be a reproduction of the rather chubby figure of the Pope after whom it is named. It is basically a thin layer of pastry rolled into a cylinder with a cream and cinnamon filling and laced with sweet syrups. The upper part is made from cream sprinkled with sugar then toasted, which is thought to symbolise the skullcap with which the Pope covered the top of his head. The white paper it is served in represents his cassock.

It soon became a favourite treat of King Alfonso XIII, who tasted it at breakfast during a hunting party at the palace of his friend the Duke of San Pedro de Galatino in Láchar.

However, a controversy soon arose regarding the origin of the recipe. Some sources maintain that it can be traced to Andalusian baking traditions or even that there were actually three pastry makers (three widowed sisters) who allegedly based this recipe on a worker known as "Blanquita".

MARY UNTOUCHED BY ORIGINAL SIN

The dogma of the Immaculate Conception of Mary, mother of Christ, propagated by Pope Pius IX, was staunchly defended in Granada by its most famous centre of theology, Sacromonte Abbey, whose motto is precisely, "Mary untouched by Original Sin."

THE LONGEST PAPACY

Blessed Pius IX, known familiarly by his Italian name "Pio Nono" (1792-1878) was the 255th pope of the Catholic Church between 1846 and his death. His pontificate lasted 31 years and is the longest in papal history, with the possible exception of Saint Peter, who is considered by some to have held the office for all of his 37 years. In 1864, Pius IX issued his famous document entitled *Syllabus Errarum*, which includes eighty condemnations of various doctrines. He propagated the dogma of the Immaculate Conception and convened the first Vatican Council, in which papal infallibility was defined for his *ex catedra* statements. He was beatified by Pope John Paul II in 2000, together with Pope John XXIII.

SANTA FE BATHS

③

• Entry free

Free baths

The Santa Fe baths contain waters with medicinal properties that emerge from a secluded hot spring discovered by a local man while undertaking a survey of the countryside at the end of the last century. People can be found enjoying the beneficial properties of the thermal waters at any hour of the day or night.

Perhaps due to the fact that they are difficult to find, these baths are "free" in every sense of the word: there is no charge for their use and no specific opening or closing hours. Nor are there any walls, changing rooms, staff or rules for bathers. Many large businesses have sought to speculate on the baths in attempts to privatise them and build spa hotels and golf courses, but they remain open to all. Due to the action of various collectives in Santa Fe, it has been possible to maintain the generosity and beauty of this site. Various alternative lifestyle community groups currently meet in the area (see opposite).

The site is surrounded by olive trees and slightly unkempt, always in need of cleaning or maintenance. The constant flow of sulphurous water at 30-34 degrees centigrade over the sloping terrain has eroded the area, creating three inter-connected ponds. These are popular with bathers, with or without swimming costumes, as well as some peeping toms. It is quite common for friends to go for early morning baths after a long night out as a group.

THE DRAGON FESTIVAL

As Spring arrives, numerous dilapidated camper vans converge on the baths bringing hippies who come every year for a festival in Santa Fe.

The Dragon Festival is a celebration that brings around 10,000 revellers to the area for a few days (never more than a week).

In fact, the festival began in the area around Órgiva, in Las Alpujarras de Granada, where there are many communes such as Tablones and Beneficio.

Problems with the authorities in those towns, and difficulties of access to Las Alpujarras, have caused the festival to move to this area, where, inevitably, it is greeted with a chorus of protests from the neighbours.

It is not easy to reach the Santa Fe baths: the only way is by car.

Some travel from Santa Fe as far as La Dehesilla. From there, they climb over dry land until they connect with the Cacín Canal service road, which joins the exit of the secondary road.

The Cacín Canal follows alongside much of the route. On the way, one passes close to the Buena Vista neighbourhood on the right.

Slightly further on, we find the Chimeneas road, which must be crossed carefully, before continuing along.

After continuing for a good while, we reach a point where we cross a ravine. A short distance further on, the Cacín Channel passes above. From here one can reach a track on the left which descends to the ravine.

HURTAN CAR FACTORY ④

Old Malaga Road, km 444 (extension of Avd. de América, s/n)
Santa Fe
• Tel: 958 511 678
• www.hurtan.com
• E-mail: commercial@hurtan.com

> ### *Luxury made-to-order roadsters*

The Hurtan car factory is the only handcrafted luxury car factory in Spain. The majority of their 1950s-style sports cars are shipped directly to the United Arab Emirates as well as northern Europe.

In order to purchase a car, you must put your name down on a waiting list and be patient as only 60 Hurtan cars are created every year. The production of one car involves 300-500 hours of work (almost six months) for the fifteen employees of this small specialist factory near Granada.

The dealership is located next to the factory in the outskirts of the village of Santa Fe and although they only work to order, it is possible to visit without prior reservations.

Hurtan cars are roadsters, with seating for two or four passengers, but they have the motor, brakes, suspension and steering of a Renault Clio, calibrated according to the requirements of their clients. A total of 400 units have been manufactured since 2004, when the Hurtan brand was established. The Hurtan Albaycín is the flagship model, with a price that varies between 37,000 and 75,000 euros, depending on the exact client specifications.

The car is ordered from a catalogue and clients can choose the type of leather for the dashboard, the hub caps, petrol tank cap (ordered from the supplier of the legendary Morgans) and even whitewall tyres and roof covers or detailing in wood. In order to adjust the seats, the client's leg measurement is taken to calculate the distance required to reach the brakes.

TOBACCO EDUCATIONAL CENTRE

Vial de la Vega, s/n
- Tel: 958 432051
- Visits possible with prior reservation in the Town Hall of Vegas del Genil
Belicena, La Vega

*Adiós
tobacco*

Among the former brick-and-wood tobacco drying barns built in 1953, there is an Educational Centre where you can learn about traditional tobacco farming and explore what was a very significant industry in La Vaga de Granada until quite recently.

For centuries, tobacco production was the principal activity in La Vega de Granada and now a museum has been dedicated to this aspect of local history. Tobacco farming has declined in recent decades, yet the beautiful and simple drying barns have remained. Some of them have already been declared sites of great cultural interest.

The drying barns used by the Educational Centre are humbly built, but it is worth seeing the restoration, which has been completed with great effort despite a lack of funds, which also makes it impossible to welcome the public on a daily basis. After the visit, you can explore the incredible site of La Vega as well as other drying barns nearby.

Some of the drying barns comprise a single surface on one floor with openings in the walls for the air to dry the hanging tobacco leaves inside. They are covered with trunks of black poplar, brick, brass or tiles and inside hold lines with bunches of tobacco leaves hanging upside down.

The enormous green leaves, knotted in bunches with grass ropes, drying in the sunshine, allow one to contemplate a faithful portrait of the region's splendid rural past. There were times when tall tobacco plants and the brick chimneys of the sugar beet factories decorated all the countryside around La Vega.

The abundance of water and the fertile soil of the plain, nourished by the Beiro, Darro and Genil Rivers, form the basis for this ancient cultivation. The watering system established by the Arabs was used with very few changes until the end of the 20th century.

The leaves would hang to dry for 10 days in order to facilitate their processing into shredded tobacco for the production of cigarettes. Tobacco would be planted in May and harvested at the end of summer.

Despite the fact that tobacco is now imported from other countries, a few workers can still be seen in the plantations in Belicena, Churriana de la Vega or Santa Fe, where they continue to farm a small tobacco field next to cornfields or land dedicated to sunflowers or barley.

BUST OF THE BOY WITH THE BIG HEAD

Plaza de las Cabras
La Gabias

> **An offensive lack of proportion**

I n 2011 a sculpture was unveiled in the main square depicting the full size hydrocephalic head of Manuel Fernández Baena, better known during his lifetime as the Boy from Las Gabias.

The Boy from Las Gabias made the town and its notoriously stubborn inhabitants (known for having "big" – i.e. stubborn – heads) famous within the province and beyond. People would joke about anyone with a large head or a stubborn personality using the expression "you're more stubborn – i.e. your head is bigger – than the Boy from Las Gabias". However, the monument also recalls the bitter story of the suffering of a young boy whose neighbours ridiculed him because of his large head.

The most striking aspect of the bust by Javier Casares is that it is made to scale, reproducing a cranium of 2,760 cubic centimetres (double the average and only 15cm less than the largest known cranium in the world, belonging to a Peruvian). After Manuel's death in 1917, his skull was donated to the Anatomy Museum of the Faculty of Medicine in Granada. Today, it is a source of pride for the town, so much so that even one of the figures of Granada's Corpus Christi procession is based on him.

According to all probability, Manuel should have been stillborn. But through good or bad fortune, he was born in 1868 and survived to the age of 49. Throughout his life, he was obliged to suffer the looks, comments and laughter of neighbours and visitors who would see him trudge through the town selling lottery tickets or begging. It was impossible for him to hide his disproportionate head.

Around 1900, the Faculty of Medicine made permanent arrangements for him to receive a pension to ensure his basic needs were looked after, on condition that his family would donate his head to science after his death.

Hydrocephalism seriously diminishes mental faculties but in the case of the Boy from Las Gabias, his hydrocephalism was partial, which allowed him to live longer. In such cases, patients usually did not survive infancy. Nonetheless, his facial features always remained those of a young boy.

ROMAN BAPTISTERY

Las Gabias
Access: Take Gabia (Granada) road from Granada to Motril and turn right at km 3.
• Visits subject to prior arrangement with the owners (ask for them in town).

> **The only Roman baptistery in Spain**

Only seven kilometres from Granada, in the village of Las Gabias, we find the only completely preserved Roman baptistery that exists today in the Iberian Peninsula. Over the years it has been neglected and even today there is no organisation between local government and the eccentric property owners, known locally as the "Toleos".

Arrangements for a visit must be made through them and they offer rather amusing and original tours.

In 1920 a local worker who owned the land accidentally uncovered the first indication that there was something under the ground. He excavated and found a subterranean crypt. Only the false vault that covered the central area could be seen on the surface.

He also found a long access corridor made from local stone and an inner room where baptisms were celebrated at a small octagonal font. The central room below the vault is illuminated and a small tower with a spiral staircase completes the structure. News of this important archaeological discovery spread like wildfire but the proprietors have always claimed ownership of the monument.

In 1922, a more systematic excavation was undertaken. Without due controls, however, this resulted in the disappearance of the decorative remains that were found. Another excavation in 1979 provided more information about the monument, which has since been subjected to some dubious restoration work by amateur enthusiasts.

The structure cannot be dated with certainty as the early Christians of Granada may have used a religious site from a previous period, although the latest studies indicate that it was used in the Byzantine era, from the year 554. In 1931, due to its great archaeological significance, it was declared a historical and artistic monument. In 2002 it was named an Asset of Cultural Interest, giving it legal protection that extended to the surrounding area, where the remains of a large Roman villa have been found. Further excavations are planned for the future.

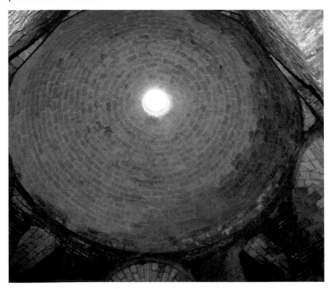

CHAPEL OF SAINT VINCENT THE MARTYR ⑧

Calle Real
Plaza of the Santo, 4
La Malahá
• To visit, ask at the bar managed by the son of María "of the saint" ("la del santo")
• Entry fee: Optional donation

The saint of La Malahá

In the town of the La Malahá, a surprising 19th-century mummy that rests in a private chapel is venerated by locals as the incorrupt body of Saint Vincent the Martyr. Dressed in roman attire, some believe that he is actually a nobleman from the past who once lived on the site.

However, the most widely accepted theory is that the relic was purchased from the Vatican by the Sánchez Mocho family in exchange for a small donation and taken from Italy in pilgrimage. It was an object of veneration in the churches and the sites that they passed through and various bishops granted prescriptive indulgences.

According to the locals, this is the body of Saint Vincent the Martyr of La Malahá (a saint that doesn't appear in any official compendium of saints), who can be seen reclining on some pillows, holding a sword in one hand and a pen in the other. The room is decorated with *ex votos*, various Mudejar decorations and an enormous painting of the Lord of the Good Death.

The rectangular room on the ground floor where the mummy of La Malahá is on display can be reached via a door from the entrance hall. It is connected to the exterior by a window, which facilitates oration from the street. The owner of the house, Rafael López, bought it from the Marquis of Alhendín, whose coat of arms graces the lintel of the principal façade. The owner seems proud to have this "holy" relic in his home and enters into rather unfair competition with the nearby parish church, fighting over the faithful who come to admire this "sacred" relic.

ROMAN BATHS

Near the town of La Malahá there are some thermal pools, built next to the secluded Roman baths, where locals have been going to bathe at all hours of the day and night since ancient times.

THE ROMAN SALT FLATS

The salt flats in La Malahá (780 metres above sea level) are located along the Salado River at the foot of Almenara Hill. Indeed, the name of the town (Malahá) has its etymology in the nearby salt flats (from the Arabic *al-mallaha* or Salt Farmhouse).

ARCH OF THE HOUSE OF THE CHICKENS ⑨

Pablo Neruda, s/n
Lancha del Genil

> *Mr Goupil's Nasrid arch*

The 15th-century Nasrid arch at the enormous villa that rich French industrialist Adolphe Goupil had built next to his gold mine was originally from one of King Muley Hassan's (Mulhacén) summer homes.

According to the most recent discoveries, the door was built to adorn an ancient farmhouse, known as the House of the Chickens because Christians found more than 1,500 chickens there when they took possession of it during the Reconquista. It is also called Dar al-Wadi (House of the River), Dar-al-Huet or Daralgüit and was one of the many rural estates that belonged to the Nasrid ruling family. The palatial home is currently being studied through an archaeological excavation.

At the end of the 19th century, the Parisian impresario placed the door with its Nasrid arch in its current location. An art collector, Goupil took the door to his home, where it remained in storage for decades until it was rediscovered at the end of the 20th century and its rightful worth was recognized.

The iron arch, crowned by a crenelated lintel, no longer has the doors once closed to passers-by, nor the hinges that once held them.

It is surprising to find an Arab arch in a neighbourhood so far from the old town of Granada, so out of place among the modern detached family houses that surround it.

No one could imagine that this gate, which today leads nowhere (it is currently in the middle of a road), was once part of two palaces, the first Arab and the second neo-Arab in style.

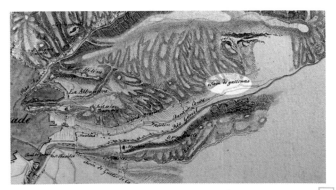

MILL HOUSE

Park of the Mill House of los Aragones, Tras Tower, s/n - Monachil
Town Hall of Monachil
• Telephone: 958 301 230
• E-mail: cultura@monachil.es
• Open: Mon-Friday 10am-2pm
• Visits must be organised in advance with the Cultural Office of the Town
Hall of Monachil

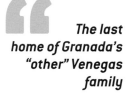

The last home of Granada's "other" Venegas family

In a large, mysterious manor in the centre of Monachil, visitors can learn a little more about the less well-known branches of the Venegas family of Granada, the heirs to the Nasrid royal family who have remained in the area for centuries. Strictly speaking, Monachil was home to the Venegas Pintor and Pérez Valiente families, descendants of the second-born son who later married into the Montezuma family, who where descendants of the Aztec emperor.

Known locally as the Mill House, the House of the Lords of Aragón or the House of the Señoricos, this is the last noble home built in the area. Its interior (awaiting major restoration) boasts an intact mill and various outbuildings typical of a rural noble estate. Behind the main façade adorned with a lintel and a coat of arms carved in stone, the Doric columns of the ancient patio support the glass floor above. Inside the mansion hangs a picture of the Virgin that bears the following inscription: "true portrait of Our Lady of Sorrows." Within the estate, we find the aforementioned mill, with its millstones, winch and the various pulleys that transmitted the movement, as well as the olive oil press.

The complex actually comprises two homes. The older and smaller villa is a reconstruction of the house built by Alonso de Venegas in the 15th century on another site. The second building was added in 1780 and was owned by José Pedro Pérez Valiente, a wealthy resident of the town. The house was purchased at the beginning of the 20th century by the Aragón family, known in the town as the 'Señoricos of Aragón'. Everyone there knew the house as the House of the Señoricos. The complex was even occupied, over the years, by a descendant of Emperor Montezuma (see page 67), whose name can be seen within the family coat of arms hanging in the church in Monachil. The property was finally taken over by the Town Hall in 2004.

THE LARGE POND

Camino del Charcón, s/n
Güejar Sierra

11

> *A pool
> at the source
> of the Genil River*

The Maitena River, which runs into the Genil River, opens into the Large Pond below a nearby pergola of trees. Here, between the bluffs of the Saint John Ravine, one can view the sunset turning every shade of yellow among the groves of pine and olive trees. This is an enchanting site that was once one of the principal stops for the cable car to Sierra Nevada and today it marks the first milestone.

Every summer people gather, wearing bathing suits to splash about in the pond. After an excellent meal in the restaurant on the shore, you can take coffee in the cool shade, listen to the river burbling along just a short distance away and watch bathers enter the pool by the stairs.

There are various natural and artificial watering holes that are also worth a visit along the route running parallel to the river. This is where the cable car used to run until it was decommissioned in 1973.

The Star Path Route is an idyllic trail for walking and filling your lungs with life. There are also some camping areas where you can chat with friends all afternoon between dips in the water - a perfect activity on hot summer afternoons in Granada.

The river, which begins in the Sierra Nevada, rushes down to the dam and later continues to La Vega and Granada. On the riverbank we find the Duke's Hotel, today owned by the local Catholic diocese.

The Large Pond has some of the charm of northern European countries during the hot Granada summer. There are no bicycles or blonde tourists but there is shade and fresh breezes that are reminiscent of Garmich-Partenkirchen in Germany or a picnic at Versailles.

NIGHT HIKE TO VELETA

Agencia Sierra Nevada Club
- Tel: 902 708 090
- http://sierranevadaclub.es/
- E-mail: agencia@sierranevadaclub.es
- Hikes on Saturday at 7.30pm during winter. Departure times vary during summer. Subject to favourable weather conditions
- Reserve in advance
- Fee: 15€/person

A night at the summit

The nocturnal excursion to the summit of Veleta, the third highest point in the Iberian Peninsula at 3,395.68 m, is one of the "different" experiences that have been organised for many years from the Sierra Nevada ski resort during the long Granada winters.

The ascent in snowmobiles from Pradollano along empty ski runs to the Veleta summit is quite mad. The views are amazing and given good visibility, one can even see the lights of Morocco or the beach bars in Motril and Carchuna.

The cold is biting but the guides on this unique outing will offer you a glass of wine with tapas to help your body cope with the rigours of temperatures as low as 15 or 20 degrees below zero, which can be reached on this summit after the sun sets.

THE HIGHEST ALTITUDE DINNER IN EUROPE

Alcazaba de Borreguiles restaurant
Tel: 902 708 090
E-mail: agencia@sierranevadaclub.es
Advance reservations required, contact Agencia Sierra Nevada Club
Opening hours (Dec-May, depending on the ski season): 8:30pm-10:30pm
On Saturdays when there is night skiing, the cable car going up is open until 8pm. Return is by car or on skis at the time of the last descent of the cable car.
Groups: minimum 50 people
In case of smaller groups, check availability and prices
Price: from 50 €/person
Includes descent by cable car, skiing or car.

On the Veleta summit, you can eat at the Alcazaba de Borreguiles restaurant at the epicentre of the ski resort to enjoy the "highest altitude dinner in Europe" at an elevation of more than 2,700 metres.

THE REAL ORIGIN OF "VELETA"

The place name Veleta may come from the etymolocially similar "veleta" (weathervane) or it could be a derivative of "vela" (candle) in reference to its flamboyant silhouette. However, in reality, as it is a masculine noun, it probably comes from the Arabic word *balata*, a synonym of "balate", which is a very typical and commonly-used word in the Granada dialect meaning "to cut/chop". So, the name Veleta actually refers to the deep ravines that can be seen from the summit, at a drop of more than 500 meters.

THE POTATO PEACE

In the middle of the Civil War, there were tacit agreements to bombard the enemy at certain times of the day.

This was known as the "potato peace". During nocturnal hours, the soldiers could enjoy themselves while the enemy crossed their lines to scavenge for mountain potatoes buried in pits to prevent them from freezing. There was a kind of pact to leave the scouts alone when they went out at night to gather potatoes.

Sometimes nationalists and republicans would bump into each other in the same pit searching for potatoes by moonlight.

CIVIL WAR SHELTERS

During the summer, thaws remove the usual 2 or 3 metres of snow that cover the summit. At a height of 3,100 metres one can clearly observe the Veleta Positions, ancient military parapets which serve as reminders of the Civil War. They were used to monitor the Alpujarra Pass (republican) from the north (nationalists).

There, on the Veleta summit, the Thirteenth Dombrowski Brigade Unit was established. They were a group of international soldiers who, following the republican defeat in Malaga in the 1930s, unsuccessfully attempted to re-conquer Motril.

They reached the Sierra Nevada through the Alpujarra Pass. In Trevélez, they

contained the nationalists who were obliged to withdraw to the Mulhacén summit. The international brigade created a fierce front at an altitude of 3,100 metres but the intense cold made this location little more than a strategic position. There was only one confrontation on the Veleta summit at the end of July 1936.

During the Franco regime, the resistance movement, especially the Yatero group, armed with 300 men in its moments of greatest strength, also made use of these shelters with tiny windows that allowed them to monitor any enemy movement from on high.

THE MARQUIS OF MULHACÉN

In 1870, General Ibáñez Ibero, the Marquis of Mulhacén, began making geodetic studies using the visual connection of the Mulhacén peak (Sierra

Nevada) and Tetica peak (Sierra de los Filabres) with two other peaks in Argelia. In order to undertake his project he had to transport equipment by donkey or even by ox-drawn carts. He created trails in the sierra and camps for scientists and soldiers, some of which are still standing. He invented the "Ibáñez device" to measure basic geodetic triangulation and encouraged the preparation of a topographical map of Spain with a scale of 1:50,000.

ALPHABETICAL INDEX

ALPHABETICAL INDEX